A Sanctuary of
Their Own

Critical Perspectives Series
General Editor, Donaldo Macedo, University of Massachusetts, Boston
A book series dedicated to Paulo Freire

A Sanctuary of Their Own

Intellectual Refugees in the Academy

Raphael Sassower

ROWMAN & LITTLEFIELD PUBLISHERS, INC.
Lanham • Boulder • New York • Oxford

ROWMAN & LITTLEFIELD PUBLISHERS, INC.

Published in the United States of America
by Rowman & Littlefield Publishers, Inc.
4720 Boston Way, Lanham, Maryland 20706
http://www.rowmanlittlefield.com

12 Hid's Copse Road
Cumnor Hill, Oxford OX2 9JJ, England

British Cataloging in Publication Information Available

Library of Congress Cataloging-in-Publication Data

Sassower, Raphael.
　A sanctuary of their own : intellectual refugees in the academy / Raphael Sassower.
　　p.　cm.—(Critical perspectives series)
　Includes bibliographical references and index.
　ISBN 0-8476-9842-4 (cloth : alk. paper)—ISBN 0-8476-9843-2 (paper : alk. paper)
　　1. Education, Higher—Social aspects—United States. 2. Education, Higher—Economic
aspects—United States. 3. Education, Higher—Aims and objectives—United States 4.
University autonomy—United States. I. Title. II. Series.
LC191.9.S28 2000

　　　　　　　　　　　　　　　　　　　　　　　　　　　　　　99-089684

Printed in the United States of America

♾️™ The paper used in this publication meets the minimum requirements of American
National Standard for Information Sciences—Permanence of Paper for Printed Library
Materials, ANSI/NISO Z.39.48-1992.

To my daughters, Dani and Becky,
who still believe in the promises of the academy

Contents

Foreword

DONALDO MACEDO

While rereading Raphael Sassower's illuminating book *A Sanctuary of Their Own: Intellectual Refugees in the Academy* in order to write this foreword, I came across a *Los Angeles Times* editorial that highlights the insidious anti-intellectualism in higher education that, according to Sassower, gives rise to a form of "ambivalence [that] confuses both potential students who are unsure about the value of education except in monetary terms and academic administrators who perceive themselves as institutional managers rather than custodians of the life of the mind."

The *Los Angeles Times* editorial bemoans "[w]hat district officials forgot in 1998 and what they need to bear in mind when they meet Wednesday are one in the same: The key to the district's success lies in compelling [university] campuses to teach the skills that today's economy demands."[1] Simply put, higher education's raison d'être is to serve the imperatives of the market that embrace a language that celebrates accountability, privatization, and competition while relegating democracy, ethics, and intellectual life to the margins of higher learning. Thus, as Raphael Sassower's book convincingly argues, the life of the mind has, for all practical purposes, succumbed to the dictates of technicism where "all ideas about renovation of

ix

our infrastructure, and even about education and health care, are evaluated mainly for their utility in helping us 'compete in the world economy.'"[2] In fact, our thinking and imagination are often straitjacketed in a utilitarian capitalist competition that prevents us from learning about important and successful experiments and experiences that give primacy to democratic ideals, the life of the mind, and social justice. The present discourse on higher education not only brooks no discussion outside the narrow utilitarianism of the market economy but dismisses those who argue for ethics, democracy, and social justice as naive idealists who have not outgrown the 1960s.

A fundamental question that is rarely raised in the current higher education debate is how can universities and colleges provide leadership in the process of educational reform that stresses the life of the mind, since they are, by and large, responsible for the creation of what Senge accurately calls a school culture that is "subject to crippling learning disabilities."[3] Given the complicity of higher education in the deintellectualization of the academic culture, we need to ask the following:

- Can higher education institutions that function as cultural reproduction models create pedagogical spaces to prepare citizens who will be agents of change and who will be committed to invest in the life of the mind?
- Can higher education institutions reconcile their technicist and often undemocratic approach to education with the urgency to democratize our civic and institutional life?
- How can higher education institutions that have been accomplices to the deintellectualization of education create the necessary pedagogical spaces that will give primacy to the life of the mind?

The paradox is that although many universities and colleges have been "crippled with learning disabilities," they are expected to play a major role in the reform of higher education. Many institutions of higher learning concentrate on reproducing values of the market designed to maintain the status quo and maximize profit while deskilling students through a labyrinth of how-to skills development courses devoid of any substantive intellectual content. When content is incorporated into courses, it usually is disarticulated from other bodies of knowledge via specialization that produces, in the end, a form of intellectual mechanization. Universities and colleges cannot succeed in preparing students for a life of the mind if they continue to advocate for the vocationalization of education presented in neatly packaged instructional skills development programs that are promoted as the panacea for difficulties students face in the acquisition of prepackaged knowledge. The deskilling of students is "further complicated by the fact that schools are presently organized around an industrial model rather than informational model. Schools are traditionally organized to produce young people who are capable of working in isolation and taking direction. . . . The role of the school today is such that it attempts to extinguish the natural desire of people to gather, be inquisitive and interact."[4]

Against this landscape of technicist education that unreflectively embraces skill development approaches disarticulated from other bodies of knowledge, Raphael Sassower's book is not only timely but correct in asking if schools are able to educate "our youth to become thoughtful and critical citizens." Unfortunately, one can easily argue that more and more universities and colleges are either unwilling or unable to prepare students to become intellectuals able to assume leadership through independent thought and action. With rare exceptions, universities and colleges do not offer pedagogical spaces where students can engage in the development of a critical attitude informed by a praxis that involves both reflection and political action. It is, thus, not surprising that the present discourse concerning higher education reform remains at the cosmetic level, dislodged from the intellectual reality that necessitated the call for reform in the first place.

Among the many higher education reform proposals that deform, Raphael Sassower's book *A Sanctuary of Their Own: Intellectual Refugees in the Academy* represents a beacon of hope for all those intellectuals who revere the life of the mind and refuse to be robbed of their "aspiration to have an intellectual arena wherein not all academics are teachers and educators who are limited to the indoctrination of one generation after another." Raphael Sassower not only denounces higher education models that produce a form of literacy for stupidification, but he eloquently calls "on legislators around the nation to protect the universities in their districts as if they were military installations whose mission is to protect the future of its inhabitants. I would urge them to bring the same passion they engage in military industrial complex, a complex that I perceive to be similar to a welfare program, but with the caveat that it also enriches a small number of corporations. The price of one bomber could finance the entire system of higher education in any state; multiply by fifty, and the entire national system of higher education can thrive."

A Sanctuary of Their Own not only argues that institutions of higher education need to decouple education from the imperatives of the market economy, but it also makes a convincing case for the life of the mind, which is fundamental to the ideals of social justice, ethics, and democracy. After reading this important book, it becomes clear that the safeguarding of democratic ideals rests more on the creation of an educated, smart, and critical citizenry than on the creation of smart bombs.

NOTES

1. "Colleges Must Meet Area Needs," *Los Angeles Times*, 4 January 2000, B6.
2. Jeffrey E. Obser, "Even in the U.S., Ideology Infects Language," Letter to the Editor, *New York Times*, 15 July 1992, A20.
3. Cited in Peter Negroni, "The Transformation of America's Public Schools," manuscript, 9.
4. Ibid.

Preface

What is it that attracts so many students to the academy? What is it that allows universities and colleges to thrive in the competitive environment of the workplace? These questions about the appeal of higher education—about 14 million students were enrolled in over thirty-seven hundred institutions of higher education in 1995 (Weingartener 1999)—allow me to focus more clearly on the irony of higher education in the United States. We have a simultaneous (egalitarian) demand for accessibility to the halls of the academy while fervently maintaining an (anti-intellectual) utter lack of interest in education as such (the life of the mind). In the name of accessibility we have sacrificed every myth and ideal we have ever had in regard to what higher education should be about, namely, the development and refinement of enlightened citizens who will more fully participate in the affairs of the state than their less-educated predecessors.

The myths and ideals associated with this conception date back to the Age of Enlightenment in the eighteenth century, when the perfectibility of humanity was high on the priority list of its leaders. According to these ideals, every human being is capable of learning and improving her or his lot in life and thereby can more fully realize and ensure a basic belief in equality and equal opportunity. Likewise, just a small dose of enlightenment would increase the personal freedom of all humans, freeing them from the shackles of state and church, from the dogmas imposed by others.

But does the University of Phoenix, for example, a for-profit interstate university, indeed follow these ideals and myths of education and enlightenment? Can this university pursue and even fulfill these ideals? Or, has this particular institution come to terms with American needs and desires more accurately than all other institutions of higher education and therefore become the model of the next century, that is, in finding a compromise position between the Enlightenment ideals and current realities? As I answer these, and many other questions within this book, it will become apparent what trade-off is expected within the next generation of students and teachers. Once the trade-off is described and critically analyzed, we may become better informed as to the future of our culture, only part of which is based on and dedicated to higher education.

What I call the irony of higher education that gets played out within the sanctuary of the academy in the United States can also be understood in terms of the long-standing ambivalence toward the "life of the mind" as displayed over two hundred years of U.S. history. On the one hand, we still find what Richard Hofstadter characterizes as anti-intellectualism (1962), and on the other hand, we handsomely reward those whose intelligence is used to develop computer software and hardware. Look at our own ambivalent federal behavior. There has been a commitment to higher education in the sense of the establishment of land-grant institutions after the Civil War and the GI Bill after World War II, including some government-sponsored programs (such as Pell grants) that attempt to assist students in acquiring college degrees. Yet, witness the attack on the Department of Education, commencing with the Reagan administration in the 1980s and the continued scrutiny and pressure by state legislators to reduce state funding for institutions of higher education. This ambivalence confuses both potential students who are unsure about the value of education except in monetary terms and academic administrators who perceive themselves as institutional managers rather than custodians of the life of the mind.

In this book, I wish to add my voice to those on the recent publication trail concerned with the future of higher education (beginning with Allan Bloom [1987]). Mine will not be a compassionate plea for the lost opportunities of disadvantaged youth who are under attack for being offered so-called special treatment in admission policies (a.k.a. affirmative action). Neither will this book decry the great injustice befalling our future generations because education has become hostage to economic conditions (of late capitalism) and social stratification that systematically discriminates against the poor (in Paulo Freire's sense [1972]). This is not to say that I don't care about students or about their expectations of higher education or that I have discounted their sense of the right to learn in terms of the privilege they enjoy as students. Rather, I believe that in order to make a difference for students and in order to appreciate the privileged position they acquire, we must first change the institutional framework they enter.

Therefore, this book addresses those who control the institutions of higher education—legislators, administrators, and professors. They, and they alone, must appreciate the importance of their sanctuary for themselves, their students, and the culture at large. And with this appreciation in mind, they could offer a clear platform from which a curriculum is developed and with which we can expect to enhance rather than retard the progress of the life of the mind. But in order to convince my fellow academics that we can change our cathedrals of higher education, I offer here a stark presentation of recent economic and cultural developments that will determine a new model of higher education that may not provide optimal conditions for the life of the mind. In calling for change I try to be as critical, rational, and postmodern as possible, combining in my presentation the best I have learned of the past in order to forge a revised version of the present for the future. Some may scoff at anyone trying to be rational and postmodern at once, but for me it is an occupational hazard of an academic who feels compelled to communicate across disciplinary boundaries and perhaps even with legislators, administrators, and the educated public.

Let me briefly outline the model here. Within one generation the entire academic world could split into two major components (in contradistinction to Stanley Aronowitz's model of tiered institutions [1995]). At one extreme there will be about twenty to thirty research universities, including most of the members of the so-called Ivy League and some wealthy and large state and private institutions. We may quibble over the exact lineup, but Stanford, Berkeley, and Johns Hopkins will certainly join Harvard, Princeton, and Yale. At the other extreme there will be about two to three thousand teaching universities and colleges. There are, of course, some hybrids on this continuum, such as small private colleges with disproportionately high endowments relative to the number of students they annually enroll.

What will characterize the smaller group is a research mission funded either by the institutions themselves or by government agencies and private enterprises. They may teach a bit, so that they can use the cheap labor of graduate and postgraduate students, but their main focus will be research and development. What will characterize the larger group is a teaching mission that will encompass anything from rudimentary analytic skills to high-tech proficiency that would allow all graduates to enter the workforce. There will be some interaction between the two groups, so that some mobility would be possible. For example, professors from the teaching group could be affiliated with a research institution on an ad-hoc basis, renewing projects annually and being rewarded for specific accomplishments. At times, students from the one group would transfer to the other.

This model seems appealing because it is more efficient than the hodgepodge we observe today. Faculty, students, and the public get a mixed message when they see a well-trained professor waste time in the library rather than teach another course; summers off and sabbaticals seem silly if one's mission is limited to instruction. By contrast, researchers don't want to be bothered with teaching assignments, considering them a waste of precious time that could be more effectively devoted to another laboratory experiment. We could be clear what the missions are and reduce the frustration of faculty, students, and the public alike over aspirations that are neither expected nor rewarded.

One could argue that this model robs us of our aspiration to have an intellectual arena wherein not all academics are teachers and educators who are limited to the indoctrination of one generation after another. We expect a critical mind to be inspired and inspiring, challenging current dogmas in order to present a better future. But can this be achieved in either the current model or the emerging one previously presented? Should we separate the heart and the mind and create domains of expertise that have nothing in common? Is this really what would allow the progress of civilization? For those who think that computer skills are limited to computer languages, there are many counterexamples even in the present time, when creativity and vision are valued and sought after by small start-up companies and corporate giants, such as Microsoft. Besides, what about educating our youth to become thoughtful and critical citizens? Is this an idea whose time has passed? Or, is this an idea (Enlightenment-inspired, Marxist, leftist, feminist, postcolonial, etc.) that must be revived?

In the following chapters, I will outline some particular examples of the economic pressures on higher education and some recommendations for the revision of particular curricula (e.g., medical schools). I will also argue for the need to have a sanctuary for thought and action—higher education or the academy—where there is some so-called waste that will help us maintain our humanity and save us from cultural catastrophes. I draw on my own experiences as a student, professor, and mid-level administrator in a publicly funded university in addition to written texts to explain my approach. I use my own experience to plead for the importance of combating the encroachment of the impending model of higher education. The richer we become as a nation, the more resources we must invest in the life of the mind, or the development of the intellect. But why bother with the intellect?

My answer to this question is a practical one, perhaps inspired by Adam Smith, the guiding father of classical, neoclassical and neo-neoclassical economists, as well as by Karl Marx, the guiding father of socialists, Marxists, and post-Marxists. Both thinkers believed in the fundamental importance of economics for any society. Economic conditions, however constituted, determine the development of a society. Any development can be regressive or progressive, with business cycles, ups and downs, and crises. That disasters will befall us is indisputable; what remains disputable is how to solve them.

However deterministic our worldview remains, however dependent we feel on the material and economic conditions of our age, deep down we believe that we can prevail against these conditions and chart our future as we dream it! For example, whatever forms of technology are used, their inception and implementation will have to be imagined by us and developed by us; having given us fire, the gods have abandoned us to our vices. But these are the vices of our own design, and we have the power to overcome them, to replace them with other, less painful ones. In short, we can design our own destiny. The intellectual arena plays a significant role in the design of the future of our culture and nation.

With this in mind, then, I would call on legislators around the nation to protect the universities in their districts as if they were military installations whose mission is to protect the future of its inhabitants. I would urge them to bring the same passion and political savvy to congressional floors that they use when they engage the military-industrial complex, a complex that I perceive to be similar to a welfare program, but with the caveat that it also enriches a small number of corporations. The price of one bomber could finance the entire system of higher education in any state; multiply this by fifty, and the entire national system of higher education can thrive.

If we appreciate students as intellectuals in progress and appreciate intellectuals as prophets and guides, then we should approach intellectuals with respect and gratitude. Perhaps we should bring to the discussion of the life of the mind the same urgency that we bring to the protection of the body politics. National security is better served with intelligence (understood here in multiple senses) than with guns and bombs. Personal security and happiness are likewise better served with intellectual exercises than with military exercises. If the U.S. culture spent as much time exercising the mind as it does exercising the body, we would all be in better shape. Rather than limit the number of intellectuals and universities we have to serve us, we should encourage the entire nation to transfer funds from military bases to intellectual bases so as to imagine a future more peaceful and prosperous than the current one.

I know that some still believe that the Cold War ended because of our superior atomic technology. I know that some still believe that we can police the world with our military might and impose our rules on every culture that we encounter. But in fact it is our ideas and culture that win the day, our lyrics in rock music about freedom and love, our computer programs that are copied around the world, and our movies that are of real importance. All of these packaged and highly prized commodities have a much stronger effect than any bomber or nuclear submarine. And in order to maintain our peaceful position domestically and internationally, we should invest in the intellectual welfare system more than in the military one: the returns are much higher!

Part of the rationale for this book is my own distaste for yet another survey (sociological or not) that bemoans the sad conditions under which we academics have to work. As I have said elsewhere (Sassower 1994), the academy is a refugee camp for the privileged—students and professors alike, though with different time lines, and as such we should concede that we have privileges many other workers do not have. Ever since the divine curse on Adam to labor by the sweat of his brow, we have understood human labor to be manual. But in recent years wealthy countries like the United States have added more service jobs than manufacturing ones, and thereby created a large workforce that needs to use its mind more than its muscle (in newly configured sweatshops). With this in mind, we have to learn how to nourish the mind, cultivate our tastes and preferences, and figure out what developmental paths would be most enjoyable for the largest number of citizens. Perhaps the label refugee camps, as will be shown in chapter 2, might be more properly substituted with the label sanctuary.

What I hope to illustrate in this book is the need for intellectual play and engagement, for the sharpening of the critical faculties that we all share, and for the expansion of the cultural stage on which we play. Rather than remaining parasites or gadflies (in Socrates' sense) on society's back, public intellectuals in and outside the academy (in Antonio Gramsci's sense or not) should be oracles and sages, leaders and entrepreneurs, providing visions of yet unexplored vistas. These roles will not be simply bestowed on us: we have to fight for them and prove that we deserve them! I hope this book will be a critical celebration of the role of intellectuals in monitoring and transforming social thought and structure, illustrating what benefits could be shared by all.

I wish to thank Professor Joseph Agassi for his ongoing inspiration to think and write about pedagogical questions. My very first publication as an academic was a response to a piece he wrote on education in 1985. Chapter 3 is based on long conversations we had and some notes we wrote together in 1993 concerning the responsibility of scientists. My gratitude to him remains steadfast. I wish to thank the following journals for permitting me to revise and reprint my own pieces: "On Madness in the Academy," *Journal of Higher Education* (1994) was used in chapter 1; "Misplaced Pressure: Between Bondage and Rage at the University," *Science Studies* (1997) was used in chapter 2; and "Medical Education: The Training of Ethical Physicians," *Studies in Philosophy and Education* (1990) was used in chapter 4. I am grateful to all those who subjected themselves to reading drafts of this manuscript, especially

Kristie Bergamo and Penny Peterson. My editors, Jill Rothenberg and Dean Birkenkamp, have been unusually supportive counterparts in this business where author and editor are usually at odds with each other. And finally, my own institution, the University of Colorado at Colorado Springs, has taught me more than I ever wanted to know about the management of public institutions and the confusion of administrators. But it has also been a sanctuary of sorts, granting me early tenure and promoting me quickly, and for these acts of academic generosity I am infinitely grateful.

1

✛

The Life of the Mind

THE WELFARE OF THE MIND

Let's agree that there are three major welfare systems, one devoted to medical and social care of the unemployed, the second construed in terms of national security (the military forces), and the third devoted to the training of citizens to perform menial and professional tasks in society (education). Let's also agree that we need to support all of these systems equally. Well, if not equally, at least with some method of equitable distribution of public funds, noting, with all due respect, that one B-52 bomber costs more than the entire federal support for any state university system (perhaps all of them combined). Since we are on the topic of dollars and cents, and since my concern here is only with one of these systems, namely, the educational one, what I need to do now is explain why this system deserves no less financial attention than the other two.

As an academic, a full professor of philosophy at a third-rate university, I would probably be expected to argue for the support of the academic system in terms of the sanctity of the life of the mind. Eventually I will get to this point. But before I get there, I'd like to remind all of us of the story that led to the current university system, a system whose origins date to the eleventh century. This may seem an unrelated diversion, but I will illustrate to what extent certain issues have not changed much. For example, there is an ongoing ambivalence about the role of the university within a culture—both in terms of the financial variables that go into establishing and maintaining a university as well as its political and institutional power plays. Let's start with the medieval story of the life of the mind.

What I discovered in the story of the institutionalized life of the mind is that the cultural placing of the academy has always exhibited an ambivalent commitment to the life of the mind and a perceived luxury of those concerned with intellectual and artistic endeavors. Perhaps because of this historical ambivalence, I'd like to offer an explanation of the necessity (rather than frivolity) of this part of life for the future of humanity.

MEDIEVAL STORIES

Most of us think of the academy as the place where the 1960s played themselves out, where people smoked pot and exercised free love, and challenged "authority," whatever it meant at that particular moment. It's the place where the so-called liberal professors get together to raise hell about anything that annoys them and where values are debated on a daily basis, as if anything new can be added to centuries of commentary. It's also the place where confused kids gather for a few years of their early adulthood to develop their ideas of what is right and what is wrong about the world into which they have been born. Having left their parents' home and the high school where remedial socialization is supposed to take place, they feel free to pursue ideas they have never thought about for more than five minutes. So, is this really what the university is all about? Is this really the place where radicalism is fermented and acted out? Or, is this the image portrayed by conservatives who wish to streamline the development of young minds? Put differently, is the university a place where specific skills are mastered or a place where young adults turn into mature citizens?

Phrasing the questions about the university in these terms rather than in the more recent terms of the ideological divide between "right" and "left" or between "liberal" and "conservative" (as some, like Sande Cohen [1993], do), I hope to illustrate some of the underlying issues that plague the university. Some of these issues are related to the internal ambivalence and the ambivalence of society about the role of the academy, a role for which it has come under attack ever since its inception. One of the best chroniclers of medieval universities is Nathan Schachner, who argues that there are "three all embracing institutions that characterize the Middle Ages," which he terms the "Church, the Empire, and the University" (1938, 1). Of those, of course, the only two that have retained their medieval pretense are the church and the university. The so-called empire, the monarchy, has become obsolete in the Western Hemisphere, where democracy with all its variants is the standard-bearer for political exchange between the individual and the state.

What is the university? What is the rationale for its inception? We may be surprised to learn about the rationale underlying the university during the Middle Ages. In those days king and pope fought for patronage instead of control and students and their professors had legal as well as economic power within their domains that extended to the broader social and political context. Shrewd rulers, such as Frederick Barbarossa, realized that if treated properly, the faculty of the university could induce the obedience of people in a manner as powerful as the church or the king. In other words, the professor could be as powerful as the pope in manipulating the minds of the people, perhaps even more so, because by then "science" was on his side. But in addition, there were some practical issues that Frederick realized could be significant.

The advantages that the university could afford the king or the city-state he ruled were several. First, the attraction of thousands of foreigners brings with it revenue during their years of study; second, "these notable institutions were, so to speak, jewels in his crown," and third, if treated well, their loyalty would influence others to do the same

(Schachner 1962, 46). Frederick could see the advantages of the university, not only as a source of prestige and loyalty to the ever-challenged crown but also in terms of revenues related to the very presence of students in a particular city or state. In some interesting sense, the emerging power of the university could be used as a buffer and ally for the king in relation to the pope and vice versa. Put differently, though claiming no specific authority or political force, the university emerged as an independent powerhouse with which to contend.

As far as Schachner is concerned, once kings and popes realized that the universities could also become powerful, independent entities, they tried to exert some control over them, and that is when, according to him, the Middle Ages were over (1962, 73). The independence of the university was a peculiar outgrowth of scholastic activity, becoming a secular institution with the power of logic (and eventually empirical data) to challenge both king and pope. Independence and power had to be legitimated by some authority, since divine intervention was not an option. Because the power of the word (as logic or language) was not established yet (except in the Jewish culture, which was marginal in European society), members of the university—faculty and students—had to do the work. Originally, there were two unions within universities, those organized by the teachers and those organized by the students.

The faculty knew they had to teach subjects that would be sought by students and paid for by the general public (in terms of services). This meant that law and medicine, at the very least, had to be taught; theology and philosophy were added as well, and other areas of learning developed with time. From the students' perspective, the issue was sheer bargaining power in terms of their rent and their treatment by the local population. Around 1215 the students of Bologna, who were legally considered "aliens" and therefore without rights whatsoever, felt taken advantage of by the local residents. Threatening to leave town and seek professors in other cities, they forced a change of heart by the local authorities. As Schachner explains the situation, "Bologna, denuded of its student class, would lose in wealth as well as in status; the goose that laid the golden eggs would have taken wing. An agreement was speedily concluded. Rents for students were to be fixed by a Board of four arbitrators, or taxors; two to be appointed by the students, and two by the city" (1938, 157–8). A similar situation was recorded in Paris around the same time in relation to the legal status of professors, who, like their students, were in many cases aliens in a foreign land. For the professors, though, the stake was exclusively financial in terms of the fees they could expect from their students. So, in terms of the politics of their status, professors and students fought for the same rights and sought the support of the local authorities against the abuse of the local citizens.

In 1357 the Duke of Orleans was fighting with the Duke of Burgundy. The faculty of Paris decided to intervene in this political dispute and bring about peace. The Duke of Orleans was not pleased and said, "As you do not consult knights in questions of religion, so you ought not to meddle in questions of war; therefore return to your books and attend to your own affairs, for though the University is called the daughter of the king, she should not interfere with the government of the kingdom" (Schachner 1962, 113). Just as the political affairs of the state were complex, so was the situation within the university. To ensure democracy within the confines of the university, most matters required the use of the seal of the university. In some cases, the seal was locked in a chest that had seven locks, each requiring the keys of the seven faculties. If a faculty was not consulted or if it did not agree with a particular decision, the representative of that faculty would claim to have misplaced the key and the seal could not be used. This forced consensus led to a sense of compromise that ensured that decisions were agreed to by all (Schachner 1962, 120–1).

From these stories one could get the impression that academic institutions of the medieval period were extremely powerful and that they could withstand many political and economic pressures. On some level, as we have just seen, this is true. But, as the experience in Salerno illustrates, there are cases where the overextension or pretensions of an institution can be detrimental to its survival. The university at Salerno was the oldest of the universities not only in Italy but in the Western world. Its foundation dates to the tenth century, where it became the center for physicians who trained students in the fine art of medicine, partially because the region was known for its medicinal mineral springs (Schachner 1962, 51).

The zenith of Salerno was reached during the eleventh and twelfth centuries, but its decline was evident by the thirteenth century. Schachner attributes the decline and eventual demise of this institution to the fact that it was too conservative to accept the new twelfth-century Arab medicine, holding on to the teachings of Galen and Hippocrates. Not that the old ideas were obsolete, but the new trends and herbal prescriptions were summarily dismissed and ignored in Salerno. No matter what intervention was gained by Frederick II, who reigned over Salerno and who decreed that it would have the monopoly on teaching medicine, students moved to Montpelier, Padua, and Bologna instead (Schachner 1962, 52). The insistence that academic institutions will be conservators of past knowledge does not preclude, as this story suggests, their ongoing research and scholarship of current trends and ideas. Universities have to maintain past knowledge and keep up with every facet of new knowledge, even if it turns out to be misguided. If an institution remains aloof from contemporary knowledge claims, it may fail to attract students and have to close its doors.

CONTEMPORARY RESIDUES

Lessons like these, almost eight to nine hundred years old, may shed some light on some of the confusions we still feel today in regard to the role of teachers, the power of students, and the material they are supposed to engage in while attending institutions of higher learning. Should teachers just hold on to the knowledge base acquired in their own days as students? Must the professors chase every new trend and present it on the same footing as age-old truths? Should politicians dictate which institution should teach what subject matter (as is the case with veterinary schools)? Should professional organizations, such as the American Bar Association or the American Medical Association, limit the proliferation of law or medical schools, respectively? Should students have the right to choose where and what to study? These questions are not new, but require every generation to reconsider them so that the confusion and anxiety we experience could be more fruitfully understood. Perhaps a different understanding would result in making different decisions from those made a generation or two ago.

As I said earlier, perhaps if we focus for a while on the professors, those who are the custodians of knowledge and truth, we may have a better understanding of their goals and ambitions, their expectations, and the roles they assign themselves. If we understand them better, we may gain some insights into the mysterious institutions of higher education that are governed by them. I am ambivalent as to what to label the universities. They seem to me refugee camps for the privileged (see Sassower 1994), both professors and students, for they provide a certain insulation from some of the conditions of commercialized technoscience or the postcapitalist culture. People escape to them from the harsh demands of the so-called real world, because the demands within the confines of the academy are relatively simple for the privileged. For example, if parents or the state subsidize one's existence for four to twelve years, then this is definitely a refugee camp for the privileged. As for professors, students, grants, and state and federal subsidies guarantee a certain income that remains relatively immune to the pressures of economic downfall or annual financial losses.

One could claim that it is scandalous to appropriate the term *refugee camp* for those who seem privileged, that professors need not run from any danger since no danger is in sight. Instead of this label, then, perhaps a more appropriate one would be *asylum*. This label would still have the connotation of being separate from the pressures of the conditions of modernity and postmodernity but would make it sound more voluntary—one chooses to go to college; one chooses to be a professor. One is not escaping a morbid fate when one enters the academy. The word *asylum,* of course, has also the connotation of a place for those needing protection, such as the mentally insane. Are students and professors presumed to be mentally or socially dysfunctional?

The cynics would say yes, since students and professors waste their talents on esoteric materials and fail to take advantage of their mental abilities to make a lot of money on Wall Street or Main Street. Others would also say yes, since it allows us to buck trends and hold on to unorthodox ideas without the regular penalties of commercial culture—professors are paid to say weird things! On the other hand, some would argue that students and professors are not insane at all but find a good opportunity to advance their careers and potential earning power when they join the academy for a limited amount of time in their lives. Moreover, as a short-term investment for a long-term return, the so-called asylum indeed allows all of us to escape some daily demands for a period of time so that we can be more prepared to handle them when we rejoin the real world.

Perhaps a third option might be a more suitable label for the academy—*sanctuary.* A sanctuary has all the connotations of being outside of the real world, so to speak, but does not have the negative connotations of mental insanity or escape from a sure death threat. A sanctuary brings to mind the positive image of a convent or monastery, where spirituality is sanctioned and supported not only by religious orders but by society at large. Those in a sanctuary are privileged, of course, to the extent that they don't have to worry about their survival, and all of this is in the name of living the life of the mind and spirit. Their dedication and devotion are respected and provide a constant reminder that chasing money and power is in fact secondary to the true quest of humanity: being one with the universe and god (following whatever religious or atheistic philosophic version).

I prefer to think of the academy as a *sanctuary,* perhaps because this term also adds the image of being sacred in some sense. To be sacred means at the very least that there is something special in the name of which an activity is undertaken. To be sacred also means that one should tread gently when entering the site and look around with respect and humility before one makes a judgment. Those of us privileged enough to have traveled around the world know what it feels like to enter a temple where unknown gods are worshipped. We are puzzled, yet we suspend our judgment; we observe with a tolerance we rarely display toward more familiar practices and modes of behavior. We wonder, and we listen. We try to learn before we pronounce our conclusion. Isn't this exactly what we expect an academic experience to be about?

A SANCTUARY FOR THE EXPOSED

There were two traditional sites where one could "go mad," that is, be oneself without regard to external conventions and social pressures: the insane asylum and the academy. That is not completely so, because the convent and the monastery were also in that group of sites, though their regime and discipline seem much more formidable nowadays. Perhaps the first classification may still hold if one qualifies the academy in terms of its genealogy and the strong ties it had to religious institutions. But that is all "history." That is to say, to look at these institutions historically or through the archives, à la Michel Foucault (1971), is only the beginning of the story I want to tell, retell, or just live through in the following pages. Instead of sketching a Foucauldian "history of the present" (Foucault 1971, 31), I wish to suggest a story of the future.

The academy is my focus, because it is there that I have my home, my refuge, my solace. Within the hallmarks of learning, with books surrounding me, with the languages one does not hear on the streets, and with people whose idiosyncrasies are worn on their sleeves, I hoped for autonomy and solitude, a quiet escape from the demanding bustle of social organizations, bureaucracies, and commercialized culture. But all of a sudden it seems that the academy has failed to provide its inmates with the same security and protection accorded to the so-called mentally insane. It is neither an "ivory tower," completely detached from its surroundings, nor a production line of knowledge and industrialized patents. The academy is paradoxically part of and set apart from its cultural environment. Two phenomena may be intertwined in setting this situation. First, the setting and second, the admission policy. The setting of the academy has worsened over the years, because it has become overly bureaucratized, so much so that the setting is no longer perceived as being any different from any other governmental or business institution. There is a hierarchy and an accountability system, there are budgets and policies, there are departments and tenure proceedings, evaluations and publication quotas for merit raises, tenure, and promotion. In short, the routine of the monastery is supposed to free one from worldly impositions, to liberate one's mind to spiritual activity. By contrast, the setting of the contemporary academy is so consuming that to avoid its trappings seems almost impossible. Just think of class preparation, students' paper revisions and grading, class discussion, office hours, committee work, conference trips, publication deadlines, and the pervasive (surveillance) technologies of memos, electronic mail, telephone, and personal computer, and you will see what I mean. The setting is burdensome to the extent of being overpowering, overpowering to the extent of being oppressive, oppressive to the extent that one loses autonomy and a sense of individuality. In short, one feels unable to express passion and pain and unable to be left alone as if in a monastery.

As for the admission policy, to put it plainly, there are very few intellectuals who are ready to be left alone so as to go mad or who are already mad enough to be interesting and creative. I believe that we turn away those on the edge—we don't admit them to degree-granting institutions, or we expel them for their "inappropriate" behavior—and lead them back, when they consent, to center stage, to the mainstream of thought, to the haven of the establishment of their respective fields of interest. The uninitiated few are led like cattle to the slaughterhouse so that we can slaughter their creativity and imagination, their desire and passion, their ability to transcend themselves and go mad. And when we are done, after years of indoctrination in the undergraduate and graduate programs of their choice, we coerce them, with much trepidation, into an institution that guarantees them no power whatsoever until they receive tenure some seven years later. In effect, we take young eighteen-year-old minds and strap them for the next twenty years to a harness that has the power to subdue them enough to take out whatever craziness was originally part of their inspiration. There are various methods of "subduing" the mind, one of the most prevalent is the study of quantification methods (e.g., probability and statistics) or of complex models so that the sheer mental agility expanded on their mastery leaves little room for challenging presuppositions or matrices.

You may ask why I am so interested in craziness, in the sanctuary that the academy is supposed to offer those going mad, or why madness is valuable at all. I would respond that craziness, the way I understand it (perhaps not the understanding of novelists, such as Fyodor Dostoyevsky, or psychologists, such as R. D. Laing), is a necessary component for the survival of the species and definitely a necessary, if not always sufficient, component for the attainment of happiness. I don't mean to glorify madness as in the mad artist or author who comes up with great visions and images and portrays them so eloquently as if the muse came over her/him or as if an oracle was responsible for the creation. I mean madness on a much more mundane level, but a level most intellectuals do not reach because they either erect barriers around themselves or accept the barriers erected by others against their personal voyages.

For me, *madness* and *craziness* are terms that describe the out-of-the-ordinariness, a posture that propels one to venture outside of a system of thought into another, no matter what spatial imagery is ascribed to it. It is a feeling and an orientation, an attitude and a courage that allow one to plunge elsewhere, visit other regions of the mind, and inspect where one has been before, where one is now, and where one wishes to go in the future. One can think of the legitimation (in scholarly terms) of the study of subcultures as an example. It is a way of being "uncontrolled by reason; passing all rational bounds in demeanor or conduct; extravagant in gaiety; wild." The wildness of one's mental behavior is also a condition wherein one is "carried away by enthusiasm or desire; wildly excited; infatuated" (OED).

You may call these descriptions misleading and silly, as if the mad professor is really that great and deals that well with colleagues and students alike. But, this is not so much in defense of the mad professor as it is an encouragement to all professors to be passionate—not so much because they will discover the "world," but because they might discover themselves in their wildness and excitement, in their enthusiasm and infatuation. Self-discovery, the psychologists will readily offer, is nothing new. And it does not require madness, perhaps some self-reflection, but that is all. I don't mean the reflexivity of contemporary sociology and ethnography, or the concern one has with being in touch with one's feelings. Getting in touch with one's emotions is a nice exercise, but it usually remains at the level of an exercise, something one does because one is supposed to do it. Besides, in many cases, the goal of self-reflection is "normalization," encouraging a so-called reality check, as psychoanalysts call it, and not destabilization, encouraging a reality checkout.

Instead of normalizing individuals, that is, asking them to be respectable or to not raise their voices in public (in Ernest Gellner's sense of irrational behavior [1992, 136]), there may be a need for change. The change of heart and mind can come about with thoughts and actions that are not supposed to be thought or done, that are beyond the range of reasonable possibilities offered on a silver platter to anyone within the academy. The silver platter of respectable scholarship demands incestuous relations within an ongoing debate to which each participant contributes yet another footnote to a footnote. Perhaps what I wish to encourage is the (Lyotardian) notion of inventing new discursive games or, if not inventing new ones, at least making new moves or changing the rules of these games so that the linguistic game must ipso facto change as well (Lyotard and Thebaud 1985, 49, 61). This could include the outrageousness of experimenting, committing blatant mistakes and trespassing all boundaries, deliberately upsetting norms, and challenging everything from tradition to belief, from thought to action. Perhaps this text is a partial attempt to express this attitude. An attempt like this is of course crazy in some benign sense because it may leave nothing intact or because such a process engenders destruction without reconstruction, leaving one empty-handed in some devastating way, remaining puzzled and perturbed. Yes, this is the price to pay, but a price worth paying because of the promise it holds for a different world, a transformed reality.

You may call me crazy or elitist, or say that because of my tenure I can probably afford the price but that undoubtedly my invitation to others is naive at best or even irresponsible. Of course you are right to some extent. Of course I have to ignore my own recommendation on some level. For example, certain canonical texts in the history of ideas should be studied by students, like Socrates' "Trial"/"Apology." At the same time, there is good reason to explore and experiment, read less well-known texts of the history of ideas, read literature, such as Mary Shelley's *Frankenstein*, as if it were science, or write essays for non-"professional" magazines without receiving academic credit. (This is a notorious problem for tenure and promotion cases, especially paradoxical in journalism departments.)

The voice of reason could bar potential actions and could confine us all to the cradle of rationality from which we exit only feet first. When there are exceptions, when individual academics in fact defy the rules of their games, they are in too small a minority, marginalized and patronized. You can imagine administrators saying, oh, we should tolerate a few of them, but can you imagine if all of them were like this? Besides, what would we do if all disciplinary boundaries were blurred at once? I confess that I want more out of this short and absurd life, and I want to test it in whatever ways I know, within the limits of my institution of higher learning, my prestigious insane asylum.

I can tone down my rhetoric and soften the extreme edges of my recommendation to be passionate, by suggesting the adoption of a strong critical posture toward anything that one encounters, a process whereby one is empowered to embody intellectual courage and civic responsibility. Perhaps we can remain on the edge (of that flat surface called the earth by our ancient astronomers) without falling off, without the loss that accompanies a leap of mind and faith, without, in short, taking personal risks. It may be the case that a critical engagement will bring about one's ability and willingness to challenge the most sacred of foundations, tear down the most revered boundaries of disciplinary training and career, and question the success one earns after hard labor and many years of formulaic existence.

In fact, some Enlightenment figures, from Condorcet and Kant to Jean-Jacques Rousseau and David Hume, thought of themselves as radical rebels, as freedom fighters in the name of reason for the purpose of furthering human happiness. They fought superstition and the yoke of the Catholic Church; they fought opinion and belief with logic and rationality; they were committed to bring about the revolution of the age of reason. And of course their early pronouncements were considered "mad," for they dared to criticize the Bible (in light of Spinoza) and the accepted views concerning cosmology. But is critique enough? Does it really and fully push one toward madness in the sense of courage and responsibility?

One may object that I am upholding an idealized notion of madness, one that finds its way into literary genres in ways that solicit pity and admiration simultaneously, or that I have set up a false binary between normalized and institutionalized critique and passionate madness. It is admiration that captures the academic imagination, wanting so much to be different and make an impression on others. And isn't this sort of admiration more difficult to come by when introducing a carefully constructed critique of an idea or text than when passionately making grand and vague intellectual gestures?

There is a price to pay for even the pedestrian role-playing of a critic. The critic is an "outsider" whose views are suspect and whose motives are scrutinized vigorously, and at times even publicly, so as to find their flaws and discredit them as quickly and as thoroughly as possible. The critic suffers ridicule whenever possible and the hardship and even pain of loneliness. In some ways the modern critic is like the biblical prophet who had to escape to the desert from the wrath of kings and friends. For example, Karl Marx, the champion of the working class, has been portrayed as a bourgeois supported by his friend Friedrich Engles. Thorstein Veblen and Lewis Mumford were difficult to classify in academic terms, for their work as social critics was accessible to popular culture. There is little glory and satisfaction in being an outsider, even if a respected one. And, worst of all, it is incumbent on the critic to keep the critique sharp and current, being informed of all that is changing in the culture, because it is easy to discard doomsayers as lunatics. Perhaps all they deserve, to borrow from Andy Warhol, is fifteen minutes of fame.

The critic as mad or the mad critic is not the same as the critique as madness. For the most "rational" and reasonable critique may only make its way through the efforts of mad people, those whose persistence and commitment are worth noticing or become unavoidable. But, at this juncture, a puzzle arises quickly: If critics can seem mad in their passionate delivery, and if the focus should be on critics as passionate academics, then how can one distinguish between so-called constructive and destructive madness? The emphasis here is on effects as well as on the person. Both of these issues are problematic in their own right. For example, the exclusive focus on effects leads back to the age-old concern with ends justifying their means; and the exclusive focus on persons as actors and agents of critiques brings back the fallacy of ad hominem arguments, failing to separate between arguments and their proponents. Back to the question at hand about the maintenance of constructive madness as passionate critique.

Perhaps the question is not destructive versus constructive madness, whatever such a distinction may mean, but
rather genuine and honest madness (the madness of
enthusiasm and passion, of wildness and commitment, of
creativity and utopias) and the pretense to madness. Let's
go slow on this issue, for in it are the seeds of my com-
plaint that the academy does not (but should) encourage
intellectual passion. I resort to setting up binaries once
again, those linguistic villains we are supposed to fight
against and overcome in the Hegelian sense of *Aufhebung*
or the feminist sense of a "successor science." But there are
occasions when resort to binaries is a useful way of dealing
with difficulties and of simplifying complexities. For
example, Lyotard's use of the binary of sophists and
philosophers illuminates certain problems in the legitimation processes undertaken in the history of ideas (1984). I
don't believe the complexity of intellectual courage and
civic responsibility can be laid to rest or fully articulated in
one brief effort, but taking a stab at it is always helpful: it
can illuminate possibilities as well as demonstrate dead
ends. Whichever the case, the effort of a story of the future
is not wasteful.

INTELLECTUAL "MADNESS," A.K.A. CREATIVITY

What does it take to be honestly passionate in the academy? I refrain from setting this up as a general discourse
on passion and its relation to intellectual madness, for this
is not a clinical report in any sense of the word. And it is
not a report on the etiology and stages of "professional
melancholia," a progressive emotional disorder that may
lead to drug and alcohol abuse (Machell 1988, 9). I guess
what I am concerned with is the conditions under which a
"positive" sense of madness permeates the life of the academic fully and honestly. So, rather than indulge in the
psychosociological literature that compares the academic
personality with a professional and "normal" personality
outside the academy, I will use a so-called phenomenolog-
ical approach. This approach describes an acute sense of

confusion, the kind that comes about because one feels one knows too much, not too little, and things don't match up as conveniently as they should. For example, after "mastering" the intellectual genealogy of Kant-Hegel-Marx, I needed to reconsider that genealogy in terms of Friedrich Nietzsche and Michel Foucault, Jean-Francoise Lyotard and Jacques Derrida, not to mention Stuart Hall and Donna Haraway. But even with this expansion, I was still confined to the theoretical components of the history of ideas.

The approach I prefer, however defined, does not describe just a sense of temporal loss of control or disillusionment (Mooney 1989); instead, it is a view into an unavoidable and ever-widening abyss! For instance, social theorists grasp the importance of structuralism, only to be faced with poststructuralism, deconstruction, and postmodernism, not to mention the various feminisms that permeate contemporary critiques. This might all sound melodramatic or esoteric to nonacademics. But perhaps this will explain the sense of a shattered intellectual reality or foundation that confronts most academics sometime during their career: it is a sense of the self that challenges the neat academic categories that present themselves as credentialing certificates, degrees, and publications. By the end of the twentieth century, it is also a sense of an academic self that is no longer secured within a definite disciplinary boundary, as fields shift emphasis and reconceptualize themselves (e.g., biology and chemistry become biochemistry, sociology and communication become cultural studies). What does it mean to be a professor of sociology? How does a professor of philosophy define the mastery of the field?

As disciplines change, so do academic programs and personal allegiance. The "spectator" is indeed a "participant" that must account for his or her own participation in the process of establishing the field over which mastery is claimed (Toulmin 1981). And the participation, as Elspeth Probyn claims, should not be passive: "Central to the technologies of the self is an attention to the passion of knowledge, a passion which does not reify knowing but rather entails a probability that one occasionally will lose oneself, only to find it in another place, caught up with other knowledge and people, in the reflection of another angle and perspective" (1992, 509). Now, of course, losing oneself is perhaps too much to expect from academics whose lives have been modulated into the framework of rationality, having been professionalized and normalized through the rigors of the (academic) marketplace. But, is the avoidance of passion for the sake of reason not a presentation of ourselves as disembodied ideas and arguments (as feminist critics make patently clear)? Have we lost ourselves completely? Can we do so even when we try? Stuart Hall answers that "[a]utobiography is usually thought of as seizing the authority of authenticity. But in order not be authoritative, I've got to speak autobiographically" (1992, 277).

From discussing the great potential for "going mad" in the academy, I have moved to discussing the loss of self when passion plays a role in the academy, the passion to be moved by ideas and material conditions and the passion to bring about social and political change. Passion is equated with madness in forensic psychology when one speaks of "crimes of passion," which permit an insanity plea in courts of law. But passion is also self-expression, the way in which we identify personality traits that remain hidden under the facade of reason and rationality. So, perhaps the next move is toward a notion of autobiographical authenticity, one that authorizes itself in the process of unfolding its stories or narratives.

Narratives are problematic, as Lyotard reminds us (1984), because the tendency is to view them as "grand" narratives, that is, as stories that explain everything. Not only do narratives seem to provide wholesale explanatory frameworks, but they also tend to justify or legitimate a particular viewpoint. Incidentally, this is an issue raised already by Marx in his critique of classical political economy, considered by him to be an ideological move by the bourgeois in the name of science. Marx perceived Adam Smith as someone who added to his descriptions of how free enterprise works a way of justifying it, as the best way to handle the exchange between individuals. But narratives or broad models of the way the world works need not be Metanarrative, or large explanatory models that pretend to include everything under the sun. They can be what Lyotard calls metanarratives in the sense of providing certain connections between different models and phenomena without claiming to justify everything all the time (for more on this, see Ormiston and Sassower 1989).

As far as I am concerned, a narrative is both a personal or autobiographical account of how things are and a way to record what has been experienced. In this way I might be following Plato's educational theory of recollection that suggests that we bring to the text what we already always know. Moreover, I expect narratives to provide temporal (and not permanent) connections between selected texts for the purpose of highlighting particular issues or proposing a different interpretation of situations. This way of presenting personal experiences within a framework of a narrative or story that includes more than just the bare details of a situation allows anyone to relate to what is said. This is a way to bridge between the personal, isolated self and a larger public. When we do this, we get in touch with the experiences of other people as well and then begin to communicate beyond our limited self. This communication, whether done within or outside the confines of the university could be enhanced by passion and madness so as to express the urgency and commitment of the presentation.

From this perspective, then, it would make sense to suggest that the academy should be a model of how experiences should be presented and recorded, with enough details of the facts of the matter, so to speak, and enough passion for those who are involved in the experience. This would allow those training in the academy to appreciate how they should interact with and communicate to those outside the academy. The academy could then become a laboratory for experiments of what are fruitful and effective ways to inspire people, connect them with each other, and develop their sense of individuality and community.

Chapter 1

A SANCTUARY FOR TAKING RISKS

I hope it is clear by now that I am concerned with licensing the use of passion in the academy. In doing so we may provide the conditions under which more intellectuals would be willing and able to break the rules of the game, transgress any prefigured boundaries, and challenge the authority of their respective fields of research. Is this, then, not a question of personal integrity instead of a question about intellectual madness? If integrity is the issue, then why discuss madness at all? Perhaps the focus on so-called madness is a focus on some sort of radicalism? Radicalism, to be sure, is related to something already in place, a response to something already said. So, we are back to the question of critique.

Perhaps the 1960s are fading into history textbooks, to be manipulated in accordance with current political fashion or historiographical paradigms. Perhaps the only residue of the 1960s that is discernable in the academy is the changed dress code. Perhaps the radicalism of that period has given way to a conservative streak that implores us to fit into society and climb up the corporate ladder, to be normalized. To be normal in the Freudian and Foucauldian senses means to have internalized the cultural gaze of specific sets of norms and conventions and have them dictate our behavior. In the Kuhnian sense normal means normal science, which is related to solving puzzles within a specific paradigm or framework so that no rules are broken and no paradigm shift is expected. This is sad, if not pathetic, because I hope for revolutionary paradigm shifts taking place everywhere, for people to break rules and set new ones, trying to think outside the box, so to speak.

I am not bemoaning the current recollections of the 1960s on university campuses for the sake of remembering the "good old days" or in order to say that the students and faculty of today pale by comparison with their predecessors. Either posture will undermine my concern with mobilizing ourselves to be more engaged today, to go mad in the finest sense of the term—the voluntary and not the pathological one. Besides, any comparison between the

1960s and the 1990s may fail to account for the different contexts within which campuses were organized and mobilized then and are performing today. Instead, it may be useful to use the memories and residues of the 1960s as a starting point from which to rethink the role of faculty today and, as later chapters will show, reconsider the emerging model of the academy.

It seems necessary to juxtapose the power relations of academics and other members of society (other intellectuals and the working class, for example) to the sense of class or group consciousness that may develop within the academy. Intellectuals are caught up in expressing the cultural consciousness (in terms of class, race, gender, or ethnicity) of a variety of groups, while denouncing their own loyalties and identities or their own personality. They are bound by Enlightenment and liberal ideals of neutrality and objectivity, individuality and freedom, while recognizing the structural injustices of capitalism and democracy that defy all of these principles. They proclaim marginality while cooperating with and benefiting from the ruling elite. In this process they divorce themselves from their roles as knowledge producers and consumers, as workers in the (post/neo)capitalist arena (Merod 1987). In short, academics are guilty of trying to have it both ways: retain their privilege (as it is afforded by the protected position of the academy in the marketplace, with long Christmas and summer breaks), while denouncing any and all expressions of privilege (Konrad and Szelenyi 1979, 249–50).

I am concerned, in this context, with radicalizing the academy with an infusion of passion and critical engagement. Academics should be speaking out about issues that matter (e.g., Amendment 2 in Colorado, concerning the protection of gay and lesbian rights, during and after the 1992 vote). They should behave in ways that make a difference in the lives of students (e.g., problematizing power relations in the classroom) and affect university policies in responsible ways (e.g., involvement in budget reallocation under continued threats of financial crises). To be politically useful, radicalism must be understood as "thoroughness of method," "the application of sound reason to tracing consequences to their roots," a method that "despises all measures which do not go to the roots of things" (OED).

Perhaps it would be useful to use an example of what I consider an attempt to formulate a radical thought/action. Some years ago, I was solicited to contribute an essay in probably "the" leading journal in medical ethics on whatever topic I chose. I wrote about medical education, suggesting, among other things, the reconstitution of medical schools and the reconsideration of premed programs (more on this in chapter 4). The essay was not published in that journal or in another "leading" journal in the field to which I subsequently sent it. It found an audience in an "education" journal edited out of the University of California at Los Angeles (Sassower 1990). Was the professional journey from one editor (and referees) to another and yet another necessary? Was the rejection limited to my poor arguments or examples, my style? Of course I wish you to side with me and agree that the eventual legitimation granted to my proposals by a refereed professional journal (from a prestigious university) "proves" that my own radicalism requires either courage or a preexisting position of power. I leave it up to your judgment to decide whether or not my proposals were "radical."

Intellectual radicalism does not start with demonstrations but with a reconceptualization of the framework that we would like to alter or from which we would like to break loose. Is radicalism—in the sense of passionate engagement—not part of what we have committed ourselves to when we chose to embark on an academic "career"? Or has that career—with its technologies of normalization—alienated us to the extent of suppressing our passion, our madness? Intellectual commitment is analogous to one's voluntary commitment to an insane asylum, a sanctuary whose safety can guarantee going beyond the bounds of rationality with a great deal of wildness and gaiety as forms of celebration. We are taught that nothing should be taken for granted and that everything is open for questioning. How is this training process then translated into the process of critical examination when we read and write, when we teach and learn, when we work in the business world? Is it something we can still observe in carrying out our role as privileged cultural critics? Has our private law given us the license to imagine and create, to be gay and enthusiastic, or only to exert power over others?

If we turn out to repeat ourselves or the dogmas of yesteryear, we ought to relinquish our positions of power and look for other jobs, or at least admit that we are careerists and not courageous and responsible intellectuals. If we ever accept any idea we teach without critically evaluating it, we are not worth the pieces of paper on which our diplomas are printed. And if we ever forget that our role is to educate our students and not worry about pacifying administrators, to pose questions and not necessarily advocate answers, we might as well quit. In short, if the academy is no longer perceived as a monastery or convent wherein spiritual life—of the imagination and not necessarily of divine revelation—is protected, then why bother maintaining its privileged social position in the midst of mounting political and financial pressures?

BACK TO LABELS

Whatever label one affixes to the academy, it should be a site where bureaucratization does not have the effects of undermining its protected status. The "protection" should be in order to license *madness* and accept *passion,* understanding these terms as personal means that could potentially defy the normalization of bureaucracies (in Max Weber's sense) and the hegemony of dominant culture (however defined). Radicalism then could be conceived as intellectual passion, a courageous way to deal with civic responsibility. My advocacy for an intellectual sanctuary is a response to Umberto Eco's critical assessment that "The only place where there is a division of labor between campus and militant culture is the United States" (Hoesterey 1991, 250). I would hope that we move militant culture (in the sense of critical engagement) into the academy and show how academics can be models for handling complex problems in society and offer alternative options for the public. As I mentioned before, I expect passionate and responsible engagement with students and colleagues, with neighbors and fellow citizens. For this purpose, then, I propose a partial and critical separation, an engaged detachment that can yield speculations and results that might change the very nature of commercial culture.

My appeal in this opening chapter points to the heart of the matter for those of us who recognize that there are risks associated with the sanctuary we have come to know as the academy. The risks are not only for the professors to remain misunderstood by their students, the staff, and the funding public at large but also for their own sake as risk takers. In some respects, professors are unlike entrepreneurs who take risks, knowing full well how to hedge them and how they might lose everything they own. Professors may still keep their jobs under the rubric of academic freedom and the freedom to research and do whatever catches their fancy (as long as they still agree to teach.) But professors can, and some even do, take intellectual risks that could bring about the ridicule of their peers or society; they might say the unsayable and face consequences no different from other dissidents—their sanctuary might not protect them or give them the immunity they think they deserve.

If, as I said at the very beginning of this chapter, higher education is one of the welfare systems we ought to subsidize in an enlightened and democratic society, then perhaps there ought to be room for a sanctuary like the one described here. But this means that the culture in which we live must agree not only to tolerate these crazy professors and their silly ideas but also to support them in their mad quest for knowledge and truth. I say this not only so that the lessons of the past will not be forgotten or that we will refrain from repeating past mistakes. Rather, I say this in order to remind ourselves that the luxuries of contemporary postcapitalist society include three welfare systems, all of which deserve our equal attention; I also believe that what might turn out to be the most beneficial for the future is the academic system. For unlike the other two, its fruits are future oriented, rather than focused on the training of killers or helping the disenfranchised to survive in the present.

2

✛

The Emerging
Academic Model

CULTURAL CONTEXT

Just because I argued in the previous chapter that the educational system in the United States, especially higher education, is a welfare system, does not mean that it should be as wasteful as the other two. On the contrary, the American people expect their government to tighten controls over all government-funded institutions and organizations. With this in mind, institutions of higher education cannot escape the close scrutiny of their patrons, the public. Whether it is state legislatures or the federal government, all public-funded institutions face the pressure of tighter budgets. One of the leading questions raised in this chapter is, Can academic institutions be run like businesses?

There are those, like Rudolph Weingartner (1999), who would claim that though there are differences between corporate America and universities, there should be some similarities between the two in the sense of responsibility and public accountability. Those who run the academy might feel at times that they have duties similar to those of corporate executives, at least in the sense of budgetary accountability (for more on this, see Weingartner 1999). Then there are those who wish to exclude the academic world from the pressures of commercialized technoscience and maintain it as a sanctuary for knowledge and truth, as suggested in the previous chapter. Which should it be? Should we treat the academy as a set of institutions of higher education that owe a societal debt and face public scrutiny, or as insulated entities that deserve support no matter what they do?

As these questions suggest, I am not asking how the academy is really running, and I am not offering a survey of the thirty-seven hundred institutions of higher education, from private to public and two-year community colleges. Though my commentary is informed by the internal workings of the academy, and though one needs to know how something works before one can offer a critique, I limit myself to a broad portrayal of the emerging model of the academy. This way, I hope, those who are not academics may have some better knowledge of what is going on in the academy and why it does or doesn't deserve their continued support.

Perhaps in portraying the emerging model of the academy in fairly stark fashion, I would be able to identify some features that would indicate just how difficult the choices are and suggest what kind of a compromise we ought to be developing in the next century. I also believe that the emerging model of higher education is still influenced by the climate of anti-intellectualism on the one hand (exemplified in decreased budget allocations at state legislatures across the country), and hyperintellectualism from the perspective of the service industries (computer hardware and software) on the other. In December 1986, Evert Clark, the Washington reporter of *Business Week,* declared from the heart of the government's bureaucracy, Washington, D.C., that "as science and engineering professors retire in droves, a crisis brews." He estimated that by the early 1990s 25 percent of the faculty at Rensselaer Polytechnic Institute would leave, while as many as 52 percent of the faculty at New York's Polytechnic University would leave as well. He was describing an inevitable trend of the graying of the post–World War II minted faculty and their imminent retirement. Yet, in September 1996, Louis

Menand reported in the *New York Times Magazine* that "more than 14 percent of new mathematics Ph.D.'s are unemployed" (78). How did a perceived shortage become a glut? How was it that an expected scarcity in the supply of faculty became an overabundance? Perhaps the answer lies in the ratio between full- and part-time faculty, since there are close to one million faculty members serving in more than thirty-seven hundred colleges and universities (Weingartner 1999, 8). Close to $200 billion are spent on higher education, making it one of the largest industries in the United States (Weingartner 1999, 9).

Let's examine some old-fashioned assumptions according to which the university (or multiversity, as Clark Kerr named it in 1963) was set after World War II. To begin with, there was an ever-increasing demand for higher education, given the generous GI Bill that funded soldiers returning from the war. Second, it was assumed that the university system would increase in size to accommodate increased industrial-military needs and student demand. Third, it was assumed that increased student demand would be correlated with increased course offerings by faculty, and thereby increased demand for faculty. Fourth, it was assumed that when faculty resigned or retired, they would be replaced by new, full-time faculty. And finally, it was assumed that funding for university research would keep up with and propel the growth of higher education.

These assumptions translated into the following classical model: a progressive growth of the university; an increase in the institutional size necessitates an increase in the size of its faculty. Under these circumstances, faculty retention and recruitment is a funding priority. Labor expenses increase with a hidden assumption that budgets will increase proportionally. This model worked well for a while, as budgets (tuition, government research subsidies, and contributions) continued to increase annually. When there was a limit to tuition increase, one could always count on the government's insatiable appetite for research, basic and applied, especially in the days of the Cold War and the Sputnik space race. What has changed?

Some assumptions proved wishful thinking, while other unfortunate circumstances brought the growth of academic institutions to a standstill. The worst culprits for U.S. institutions of higher learning have been the demise of the Soviet Union (the source and target of the Cold War), the victory in the space race, and the industrial-military dominance of the United States. The warnings of the 1980s about the scarcity of faculty were as unfounded as Thomas Malthus's warnings about global starvation in the face of population growth some two centuries ago (1798/1970). Efficiency and productivity were overlooked by Malthus just as they were missed by observers of the academy who held on to the classical growth model of the university. The new model of the university looks more like this: increased student demand is met by larger classrooms (a one-time capital expenditure), and not by offering a larger selection of courses (an ongoing labor expenditure). At the same time, faculty retirement is met with relief because no full-time replacement is sought; a new source of academic labor can be more rigorously exploited: part-time faculty and graduate students (see some recent statistical data in Leatherman 1999).

You can see these changes not only by examining professional records but also by reading the popular print media. A decade after the prediction of faculty scarcity found its way to public consciousness, an odd situation was reported: "U. of California Graduate Students Strike" reads one *New York Times* headline (11/24/96), while another notes that "Minnesota's Proposed Tenure Changes Lead to Union Drive" (9/22/96). Why are graduate students striking and faculty joining unions? What promises were broken in the name of efficiency? To be efficient, that is, to spend less money for the same quantity of labor, university administrators turned away from traditional ways of organizing the delivery of higher education. Later I will outline the optimal financial conditions proposed for higher efficiency of the delivery of higher education. Is the new model indeed necessary? Will it streamline an institution that needs to be radically changed?

THE SOUNDING OF ALARM BELLS

Any talk of change might raise questions about the conditions that motivated the university to change itself. Moreover, will an organizational change bring about a change in the content and credibility of higher learning? One could even ask: Is the university under siege? Is it in crisis? The answer to these questions depends on one's definitions and cultural predispositions. As far as John Searle is concerned, "the crisis rhetoric has a structural explanation: since we do not have a national consensus on what success in higher education would consist of, no matter what happens, some sizable part of the population is going to regard the situation as a disaster" (1990, 34). The university is both always and never in crisis, because we lack a yardstick by which to measure its success and failure; the rhetoric, therefore, can be made to fit whatever alarm one wishes to sound for whatever ideological purpose.

As far as Gene Maeroff is concerned, the problem faced by faculty was brought about by their own greed and laziness, their failure to meet responsibly their academic duties: "it may be appropriate to ask some of the full-timers to start behaving more like people with full-time jobs so that not as many part-timers are needed" (1993, 12). Between these two extreme views, we may find a more fruitful analysis of the transformation of the model of higher education from the nineteenth to the twentieth century. *Higher education shifted both symbolically and practically from an expression of class privilege and distinction to the production and consumption of expert technical knowledge for the sake of feeding an ever-growing military-industrial complex.* What Thorstein Veblen observed around the turn of the twentieth century as the entrepreneurial nature of the "captains of erudition," that is, the university leadership (1918), or what Alvin Gouldner observed as the rise of the "New Class" of intellectuals and professionals (1979), turned into a rigorous credential-driven process of professionalization choreographed by the "gatekeepers of the advanced technical-managerial society," as Michael Katz calls them (1987, 167).

Whether we follow Veblen or Katz, Kerr or Gouldner, we may still wonder in our postindustrial, post-Fordist, postcapitalist, and neopostmodern culture what makes the academic setting different from other cultural settings? What is it that renders the university an institution different from all other social institutions? Is Robert Paul Wolff (1969) correct in labeling it a "community of learning," trying to retain a bit of Marxist idealism laced with utopian messianism? If we are indeed a community of learning, then as far as scientific research is concerned, we would value basic or applied research and feel compelled to exercise our collective intellectual capital in the pursuit of the love of wisdom. While corporate America insists that pure or basic research ought to be done at the university (Uchitelle 1996), it still accounts for less than 30 percent of the total research and development of Western countries (Skoie 1996, 66). But as the boundaries between basic/pure and applied research have been blurred, what remains the distinct mission of the university? Is the rhetoric of crisis in fact justified if the crisis is not about the internal workings of the university but about the undermining of its social position and economic role?

Public conception of the university's mission determines its funding potential. What must the university and its leaders do in order to gain a favorable perception and reception by a confused (Searle) and skeptical (Maeroff) public? How can it avert the twentieth-century trend toward "anti-intellectualism," as Richard Hofstadter (1962) describes it? How can the captains of erudition, who have become credentialed gatekeepers, present the best image to government and independent funding agencies and retain (if not improve) their credibility in the face of material pressures and social discontent? One way to win the favor of the consumption hungry public is to present education as a commodity worthy of consumption, if not as a shrewd investment for the future. What professional schools (law and medicine) have done for centuries, and what technoscientists have promised since the Newtonian revolution, all universities must do in the late twentieth century, namely, promise that current expenditures will produce wonderful returns. But can such a promise be kept? Does every research lead to an innovation, and does every innovation lead only to positive implementation? Obviously not. And even if the answer is yes, at what price? And even when a price is determined and is found reasonable (for example, some level of pollution for mass transportation), who will ultimately pay that price?

CONTENT AND STYLE

In recent years the university system has been asked to behave as if it were a corporation. No longer are we satisfied with broad characterizations of higher education in economic terms, such as those proposed by Fritz Machlup (1962), for example. For him, the quest for knowledge was translated into knowledge production and consumption, and with Clark Kerr it was transformed into the multiversity (for more on this, see Sassower 1995, 133–40). In their stead, we are obsessed with the latest businesslike vocabulary of corporate behavior and the management of (scarce) resources (human or otherwise). This rhetorical (if not always practical) shift in emphasis has meant for some the description of academic departments as cost centers and the demand for productivity reports, efficiency measures, and input-output analysis.

In the 1990s, corporate America has been downsizing its workforce so as to increase profit margins. University administrators claim to follow the dictates of legislators and boards of trustees and are acting as if they were corporate engineers, downsizing and streamlining. In their zeal to appear cost conscious and deliver academic degrees most efficiently, university administrators fail on two counts. First, they fail to be true to corporate ideals that would turn them into better academic administrators, and second, they fail to distinguish their institutions from corporate ones. As Weingartner describes the predicament of higher education administrators: "In order truly to rethink the role of academic administrators as corporate executives and managers, on the one hand, and faculty members as their employees, on the other, they must find some IHE [Institutions of Higher Education] equivalent to a product, on the one hand, and a quantifiable bottom line, on the other. Strictly speaking, of course, that is not possible; in particular, success cannot be measured in profit actually brought in" (1999, 123).

Assuming the corporate model, university administrators accept the corporate rhetoric and its rationale on a superficial level. For example, as Weingartner would agree, they fail to recognize what commodity they are marketing and how its quality control could increase visibility and prestige and command better prices in their market niche. In short, they fail to fully appreciate and follow the rules of the corporate game, which would have made them pay more attention to ideas and pedagogy and invest more heavily on their faculty and libraries (as product development and quality control). But even if university administrators were better corporate managers or leaders, they would still fail to admit the most important distinguishing factors that set the academy apart from other institutions of contemporary culture. Academic institutions should be devoted to harboring intellectual rebels and fermenting dissent from the debilitating effects of power and authority, may it be the church, state, or industry. As such, they should be offering a sanctuary of sorts (as discussed in chapter 1).

In the context of cost cutting and efficiency, is it reasonable to argue that there is room for a cultural sanctuary, especially if this sanctuary is expensive or requires some financial waste (e.g., books that remain on library shelves for generations at a time and are seldom consulted)? The question of waste is bothersome when it is juxtaposed against a growing concern for the poor and homeless of the same culture. Some would claim that in the era of global concern for refugees of economic and political hardships there is no room to minister to the refugees of elite classes. Balanced in this fashion, the future for academic intellectuals looks bleak not so much because of their economic well-being, but rather because of their perceived role and utility in the face of economic conditions. Admittedly, this may be an unfortunate way of presenting alternatives and balancing accounts. Instead, we may conceive of academic institutions as necessary sites from which great ideas and practical solutions may emanate, as investment centers the return from which is measured every century and not every quarter, as Robert Bates Graber suggests (1995).

THE CORPORATE MODEL
APPLIED TO THE ACADEMY

Profit maximization used to be the rallying cry of corporate America at the beginning of the twentieth century. If that meant killing some landowners who drilled for oil, as the Rockefellers are reputed to have done, so be it. Once fortunes are amassed, philanthropic foundations easily cleanse one's dirty hands and ensure eternal public recognition and gratitude. The greed associated with neoclassical models of economic activity, the cornerstone of many business programs around the globe, was curtailed at the beginning of the twentieth century only through union organizing and occasional legislation concerning child labor, workplace safety, and product liability.

But that model has become a bit old-fashioned by the end of the twentieth century. Instead of profit maximization, we speak today of profit optimality and are as much concerned with corporate survival as with human resources. We argue today that profits will accompany research and development if we are willing to look at the long run, as opposed to worrying about every quarterly report. The likes of Microsoft have illustrated that wealth accompanies a changed corporate culture rather than the reverse. Even corporate giants like IBM recognize that to have a dedicated workforce they need to extend, as they recently did, health benefits to their employees' gay and lesbian partners so that the investment in human capital is deemed as important as technical expertise.

So, when academic administrators are pressured to behave like corporations, what does it really mean? Moreover, when administrators internalize the pressure of legislators and regents so as to dictate corporate-like behavior, what do they have in mind? To begin with, it seems that no one is quite clear about which economic model they would like to emulate. Since the academy is in general a nonprofit organization, what would profit maximizing mean? Second, since there are different strategies associated with profit maximization and optimality, which set of strategies do they endorse? Third, if the corporate rage of the late 1980s and early 1990s has been total quality management, how has the pressure to become businesslike been implemented in all the academic levels of operation? Is there an equivalent in the academy to the corporate commitment that every layer of an organization is dedicated to ensuring the best possible quality of the product or service sold by that organization? Do annual reports serve this purpose? Can academic committees accomplish this task?

I raise these questions to illustrate how confused university administrators (claiming to respond to public demands—from alumni to state representatives) tend to be when it comes to the acceptance of economic models and their eventual implementation. Saying that we should be watchful of our expenditures or be accountable to those who foot the bills is one thing, but cutting budgets across the board without thorough calculations of their effects is quite another. Let me provide an example. Like many universities, my own university's budgetary needs have outpaced tuition increases so that cost cutting has been mandatory. The four-campus University of Colorado's annual budget for the academic year 1999–2000 was close to $1.3 billion, of which 37 percent came from gifts, grants, and contracts, 21 percent from tuition, and the rest from state appropriations. More than 55 percent of the Colorado Springs campus budget of about $30 million was for instruction. Even with annual raises of about 3–4 percent, we still wonder where the money was spent. What percentage of the budget should properly be spent on support units for academic instruction? How many administrators are needed? What corporate criteria of efficiency are used here? Charles Clotfelter, an economist at Duke University, argues that higher education is the only service industry in the United States that has not gone through "substantial, gut-wrenching restructuring" as compared to all other service industries (Miller 1999, 49). The problem with a major restructuring is that the quality of higher education could suffer in the process, since it would be easy to dismiss faculty and close down departments and colleges, but then what would remain of the ideals of higher education? Would downsizing mean efficiency or irresponsibility? Would a simple skill-training program suffice to inspire generations of young minds to be creative and find solutions where none were found before?

If administrators run the cost-cutting effort, since faculty are practically removed from university governance (though their numerous committees may seem to tell a different story), the only feasible cost-cutting measure must be in the area of instruction: cut down on full-time positions and consolidate disciplinary areas and departments as much as possible. Faculty, at least on my campus, are indeed powerless. Even the powerful budget committee is only "advisory" to the chancellor, which in effect means that unless it does her boding it is summarily ignored. I served on the budget committee for two years and can recall with relish bringing up innovative ideas for cost cutting, all of which were routinely ignored as too outlandish—finance office run by business majors—or impractical—public safety limited to work-study student enforcement.

Obviously one does not hire full-time tenure-track faculty members, but instead hires part-time instructors who get paid piecemeal. The University of Phoenix, one of a handful of for-profit academic institutions in the United States, is spread across the United States (more than sixty sites in thirteen states) in rented office spaces. It has more than fifty-six thousand adult students (eighty-five hundred of whom are on-line students) seeking professional degrees, making it the largest private (and for-profit) university (Koeppel 1999). It boasts of having few full-time faculty positions and a growing number of students. The ideal this university exemplifies is having one full-time tenure-track head of a department with all the rest of the faculty of that department being part-time instructors. One may hire a prominent scholar as a figurehead, perhaps shared with other institutions so as to ensure some level of credibility and prestige and divide the costs associated with such an appointment. Given the specific pay scale at my university, if one were to replace full-time positions with part-time ones, one could double productivity with the same budget, or cut the instructional budget by half and maintain the same number of faculty with the same teaching loads.

In addition, one could increase the teaching load, that is, either more courses per instructor or more students per course or both. This might require larger classrooms, but the expenditure for rooms, laboratories, and buildings comes out of a different category of the budget, and that budget (as mentioned previously) is a one-time, long-term investment. In short, our universities could have a perfectly structured departmental hierarchy with one faculty administrator at the top and many semi-employed, underpaid, and exploited instructors, all of whom are hired and get paid by the course, without any benefits or job security, at the bottom.

To some extent this model is already becoming operational in many state universities and community colleges, as Stanley Aronowitz and William DiFaizo (1995) have argued. Technoscientific proliferation and growth have changed the character and need for labor in general, and that trend has not spared academic institutions in particular. As computerized workstations and on-line instruction become more available, the need for "contact hours" (when professors interact with students face-to-face in a classroom) becomes smaller. The nightmare of yesteryear has been dreadfully realized everywhere.

So as not to present this model as if it were suitable and operational only in the so-called lower spectrum of universities and colleges, let us note that many medical schools are already part of this model. For example, in the early 1980s (and I assume this is still true today), the medical school at Boston University had very few full-time paid physicians on the faculty whose entire salary came from the medical school. The majority of the teaching faculty were either researchers on grants or clinicians paid by Boston City Hospital (the teaching hospital of the medical school) or by other private or state clinics. These physicians, then, were in fact subcontractors, but in a manner different from other academics. While most academics find it difficult to secure employment outside the university setting (some find jobs at think tanks or as part-time consultants), physicians can always earn more money in private practice by spending less time on campus. Therefore the fees that are paid to physicians by teaching hospitals are considered tokens of appreciation, valued for the symbolic prestige of association with credible clinical settings rather than for their monetary value.

Back to the organizational chart of the academic model envisioned here. Add to the departmental hierarchy the efficiency that can be achieved based on the contemporary zeal for inter-, counter-, and cross-disciplinary approaches to areas of study (proposals that unwittingly enhance academic downsizing and faculty unemployment), and one can limit the number of departments in the classical college of liberal arts to three departments: natural sciences, social sciences, and the humanities. Incidentally, this way of teaching reverts back to some of the medieval models discussed in chapter 1. Some other professional programs or colleges can be collapsed as well, so that one would streamline and simplify the archaic university structure. Five to ten departments or programs would be run by five to ten administrators, all of whom report to one chancellor or president, and that is all. No need for committees, because there are no academic questions to be debated, either on the governance side or the curriculum. There is no one to govern, if all instructors have no status in the university and are basically subcontractors who work piecemeal, and curriculum decisions are made by the head of the department or program or dictated by a national organization. In both cases, managerial authority is exclusively placed in the hands of the one and only full-time (with benefits) certified faculty, an alleged philosopher-king in Plato's autocratic sense.

To be sure, something of this sort has already taken place on most campuses as two different groups have been formed. There are the professional intellectual workers and the administrative class, composed of faculty members who have either been plucked from their academic positions early in their careers or chose themselves to leave the classroom, laboratory, or library (Aronowitz and DiFaizo 1995). They hardly published or taught, so their sensitivity to the needs of researchers or students is at best feigned or simply absent. The rift between the two groups, one with a managerial posture and the other with proletariat-like demeanor foregrounds faculty and student frustration and alienation (for more on the push to unionize, almost in the medieval sense discussed in chapter 1, see Weingartner 1999, 123–4). The small percentage of U.S. faculty that belong to unions is still puzzling. Perhaps it is the myth of collegiality and the community of scholars (or learning, in Wolff's sense) that keeps them from believing that their colleagues are turning into heartless managers whose concerns have shifted from quality education and research to input-output analysis and quantifiable results.

As for the rest of the student support system, most of it can be easily eliminated and substituted with computer-assisted programs, from course registration to advising, from financial aid to writing labs. If there are any staff positions that need to be filled on campus, they can be filled by work-study students whose pay is subsidized, in the United States, by the federal government. In short, full-time faculty members and staff will be reduced to a minimum that can save millions of dollars. As for other academic needs, such as a library, they can be reduced to some terminals hooked to the Internet and served by a couple of work-study students to process interlibrary loans from the great libraries in the United States, such as Harvard's. What else does one need? Cafeteria, bookstore, and varsity sports can all be subcontracted to independent vendors, so that the university's financial exposure is minimal.

Despite the appearance of efficiency, I would contend that business leaders would not endorse this model, and here is why. However capitalist-minded these individuals may be, they do understand one fundamental principle that turned their corporations into successful multinationals: *do not compromise on your product, do not short-change the focus and quality of your commodity.* Now, what is the academic commodity? What do we sell in universities? As noted earlier, we do not sell degrees, though they are handed over to students at the end of their studies, and we do not sell only basic skills that can be acquired through how-to manuals at any bookstore. What we sell, day in and day out, is higher education: intellectual curiosity and critical thinking skills across a variety of disciplinary boundaries. We sell the promise and hope of learning how to be thoughtful and creative, sensitive, and passionate.

Assume, for a moment, that indeed we do sell an attitude toward the life of the mind and appeal to people's intellectual aspirations. Assume, as well, that what we sell is worthwhile because it prepares people to become better citizens and more creative members of a community, whether they choose to be businesspeople, artists, or manufacturers. If what we sell is the love of higher learning, then let that be the focus of the university, and let its salespeople and spokespeople deal directly with this "commodity." Let them know what we sell, as opposed to waiting to hear from others what it is that we ought to sell. Let them be, like all others who sell their wares, acquainted with their products, the different disciplines and their methodologies, and the quality of these products; in short, let them appreciate the life of the mind.

When a microbrewery sells its beers, it makes claims about the ingredients and the process of brewing, it appeals to people's tastes and imagination, and it tries to sell its brews on the basis of quality. Have you ever heard your chancellor or president passionately discuss the quality of the curriculum in your department? Do our administrators even know what we teach or what STS stands for? Most commonly, the answers are negative. Instead, they come to us and tell us how we should package ourselves to be more appealing to the needs of government agencies and industry. Is this what Bell Laboratories has done over the years? No. They funded basic research and developed numerous products they believed in and then proved to the public how important and useful these ideas, products, and processes are. Only then did they package consumable goods and turn a profit.

Karl Marx taught us about the fetishism of commodity production, distribution, and consumption, alerting us that more often supply creates its own demand, rather than the classical (and neoclassical) economic notion that supply comes at the heals of demand to satisfy needy and eager customers. Do we need twelve kinds of soaps and a thousand kinds of perfumes? Do we need several brands of clothing? Do we, as individuals and as a culture, need education? Do we need higher education? If we fail to convince the anti-intellectual culture in which we live that more rather than less education is crucial for the survival of the species, then we are doomed to end up competing for scarce resources as if we were in the marketplace of fast food chains. Against them we have little chance to survive. The belly comes before the soul, as Marx knew from studying Adam Smith and David Ricardo.

THE IMPORTANCE OF WASTE

At this juncture I'd like to introduce a counterintuitive concept into the language of economic thinking, as it applies to the university in my model. Just as university administrators have to become passionate spokespeople for the love of wisdom, the quest for inspiration, and the life of the mind, they have to become advocates of pockets of waste so as to ensure the progress of civilization. Waste is detested by economists and business people as a plague one must avoid and extricate. But there are different kinds of waste that should be delineated. On the one hand, there is unnecessary waste, the kind that produces nothing but aggravation to all involved, the kind that gets in your way and makes everyone look bad, the kind that is best avoidable and dispensable.

On the other hand, there is useful waste, that is, waste that is defined as such only in a narrow-minded, short-term perspective, but which turns out to be useful in the long run. For example, it might seem wasteful to have two groups of researchers follow the same protocol simultaneously. Yet, as any laboratory researcher knows, what we sometimes call control groups, or what others call independent verification, is crucial in order to ascertain the efficacy of certain experiments. Do we call this waste? Buying books that are stored on expensive, temperature-controlled library shelves is an investment that makes little sense in the traditional economic model. But if these books and articles, artifacts and laboratory equipment, turn out to illustrate all the dead ends and the uncharted territories of the mind, what cheaper investment is there for the inspiration and production of different and new ideas?

Businesses in software, information, and communication technologies do not believe it is wasteful to have a group of well-paid researchers hang out and come up with bizarre ideas that might never see the light of day or the production line. They understand that if only one in a hundred of these ideas turns out to be revolutionary, it could change the way we think and operate, it could bring about a Kuhnian paradigm shift (with tremendous profits in the long run). Some ideas lay dormant for years; some find immediate buyers in the marketplace of ideas. If we narrowed the marketplace to only those ideas whose selling power is prefigured, we would never come up with new ideas. If we limited our imagination to what is already traded in the marketplace, we would repeat ourselves and never venture to change the entire marketplace.

So, my advocacy for intellectual, artistic, and academic waste is a plea for the present and the future, based on what we have seen in the past. How sad it would be if the only refuge sites were limited to monasteries, insane asylums, and defense contractors. Why not include the universities in this range of refugee camps for the privileged few? Why not support academics? They are, after all, self-motivated and quite cheap. Remember, unlike the military-industrial complex, the university has an army of exploitable intellectuals in progress called graduate assistants and postdoctorate fellows who are all too happy to sell their labor power for small wages and pieces of paper we call diplomas.

My advocacy for spending money on the university system should make sense to both government agencies and industry because of the collegial environment enjoyed at the university. The target age group is such that family planning and retirement packages are not on its members' minds (because they are still too young to worry about them). They are more motivated and open-minded compared with their more established and older counterparts because the latter group is already established and is much better paid. As such, the pressures of industry are offset by leisure time that is relatively lavish by comparison with your average graduate student. However competitive academic life is, it is relatively friendly and collaborative compared with the corporate world, where climbing the corporate ladder is more often than not a nasty undertaking.

My parting comment in this chapter, then, is that university administrators misplace their pressure on faculty and students. They may wish to pressure us all to think critically and creatively and to come up with alternatives and improvements, instead of pressuring us to save money. Small-scale seminars are not wasteful but useful; large lecture halls are wasteful because they tend to produce blank stares as if the experience were an alienated, one-sided television exchange. Fruitful instruction, the personal interaction of a team of scholars and researchers, cannot be duplicated on the Internet, and that is why even Microsoft's researchers work in a university-like setting in Redmont, Washington, and not in their respective homes, connected via modems. Technoscientific innovations may induce shortsighted captains of credentialed professionalism to replace the quest for knowledge with its production, distribution, and consumption. But human curiosity and creativity cannot be mechanized and licensed; they must remain mysterious processes that require preservation and nurturing at a price every culture should be honored to pay.

3

Intellectual Responsibility

THE AFTERMATH AS REGENERATION

While most of the attention related to ethics and responsibility in the academic community is directed toward the external relations academics have with political agencies, corporate sponsors, and military research projects, I wish to focus the attention on the internal workings of the academy as an institution for higher learning. I should hasten to say here that I do not follow some recent books (such as Hoekema's 1994, Markie's 1994, and Weingartner's 1999 concerns with specific codes of conduct or the specific duties of professors), but rather the more general context in which institutions of higher education operate. My approach is not meant to discard the importance of students in the process of transforming the university system or to dismiss the input of the general public that keeps on paying the bills of the academy (either as direct funding or indirect exemption from real-estate taxes, for example). Rather, as I have said previously, my concern is with those who have the power to change the academy from within, the professors, administrators, and regents who set policies. In order to bring about change, I suggest that we keep an eye on a cultural overview that would more fully explain why there are specific concerns with professors' roles and duties and public expectations related to them.

Academics seem to be less reflexive in examining their own institutional affiliation than would be expected of them and thereby miss great opportunities to appreciate their own predicament. Their predicament is indeed a compromised position as advocates of the status quo and the ideology of the mainstream, while trying to retain a critical stance toward their own disciplines and the institutions that support them. These observations will be linked to the previous two chapters in terms of the emerging model of the academy. This model would tend to put more pressure on academics to perform some duties that go beyond the teaching responsibilities to which they agreed when embarking on a life-long path of research and publication.

As far as I can tell, there are pressing issues that face academics in addition to the mastery of their field of research and their commitment to teaching. These issues emanate from the horrors of World War II, when many of the Enlightenment ideals of perpetual peace and the education of humanity were shattered. After Auschwitz and Hiroshima taking stock is imperative not only of the negative effects of technology but of all other events that bring us up to the end of the twentieth century. It is not that science and technology stand alone as the culprits of that era, but they have come to determine and define the twentieth century and all the unexpected effects it has had on human progress. The cooperation between science and technology seems obvious, and the gulf between science and religion seems unbridgeable and obvious too. Yet it is unclear, even unknown, what of science and scientific technology is preserved and how, when it is transferred from one culture to another—laterally or longitudinally (that is, from one generation to another or from one country to another during the same generation).

The issue here is that of the responsibility of (self-appointed) intellectuals to speak out critically about the preservation of science and of scientific technology and to do so self-reflectively. The self-reflective move is incumbent upon intellectuals, for at least the following four reasons. First, quick and narrow response to horrendous events such as Auschwitz and Hiroshima may miss too much, for example, the cultural settings of these horrendous events and the fact that Germany at the time was in the zenith of its cultural development as no other European country was. Second, a hurried response may overlook the culpability of intellectuals themselves as the self-appointed guardians of the flame of the Enlightenment or as the self-proclaimed cosmopolitan messengers of its torch. Third, until intellectuals take a critical look at these horrendous events and begin their research programs with Auschwitz and Hiroshima as significant intellectual matrices, there is no reason to trust that the twenty-first century will turn out to be any better than the previous one. Fourth and last, responsible response invites the examination of the universalism that justifies the cultivation and preservation of science and not only the nationalism that is deemed obviously problematic for those concerned with the cultivation and preservation of science.

In light of all of these issues, I suggest that a discussion of the transformation of science and technology must be central to a discussion of the academy and its cultural role. Intellectuals as cultural critics ought to reconsider the promise of a world peace that is offered by enlightened and humane pluralism, a pluralism that preserves science as relativized critical rationality well within culture. And as part of their cultural duty, they should offer ideas and suggestions of how to solve potential problems related to technoscience. Inspired by Joseph Agassi's views, I plead here for a process that requires a certain mind-set, as if preparing the ground or setting the stage, for a critical performance to begin. The problem is how to awaken this latent psychological predisposition, such as assuming personal responsibility for cultural phenomena and behaving in a manner that displays the commitment to playing the part of an integral detail of the society in which one lives, so as to enhance critical self-reflection. One obvious condition that constitutes a ground, necessary but not nearly sufficient, for launching the cognitive-cum-psychological process of self-criticism, is courage.

SCIENTIFIC KNOWLEDGE AS A CULTURAL VALUE

The standard distinction between scientists and technologists is that while the scientists engage in theoretical activity, technologists' concern is practical. Technologists
depend on scientists to supply them with science to apply,
as their job involves applied science. This distinction is
conveniently used in order to contrast the claims associated with science and technology (and at times misused in
order to shield science or technology or both from public
scrutiny and control). For instance, it is convenient to propose the complete freedom for scientists as the proposal
for the complete freedom for scientific research, because
science is theoretical and thereby benign by definition. By
contrast, it is common to propose close control and governmental regulations of the conduct of technologists, of
anything technological, because technology is assumed to
be practical and thereby potentially dangerous; this too is
so by definition. As I have argued in relation to the Manhattan Project (1998), the convenience of employing this
rather strict distinction between scientists and technologists is suspect, even when we fully endorse the strictest
distinction between science and technology. For the activities of theoreticians may turn out to be technological and
dangerous, while ever so many practical activities of technologists remain benign. Moreover, distinct as science and
technology may be considered, obviously, they have to
cooperate. Some scientific discoveries owe their very existence to the aid of prior technological innovations, and
these, in turn, were at times inspired by speculative ideas
of theoreticians, called scientists or natural philosophers.

Nowadays some students of scientists and their practices, for example, Bruno Latour (1987), use the term
technoscience in order to be explicit about their interest in
the society in which scientists and technologists interplay
in instituted systems of association. This term, though, has
it roots in the Pentagon lingo of post–World War II
(research and development, better known as R&D), and
has been applied primarily to what some call the military-
industrial[-university] complex. This complex is consti-

tuted with the intent of employing as many scientists and technicians as possible at relatively cheap costs. This can be accomplished at their home institutions, with local state support and the tuition collected from unsuspecting parents and independent students alike. The first experiment at central planning for Big Science was the successful design of nuclear weapons, accomplished, as mentioned previously, in the Manhattan Project. While involved in the Manhattan Project, scientists and technicians were confined together in Los Alamos, New Mexico, in order to thwart the Nazi threat and for the explicit purpose of designing an atomic bomb (used, after all, against the threat of Japan rather than Germany).

Now, the organization of technoscience of post–World War II is no simple matter and cannot be solely studied in nationalist terms. It deviates from the law of the United States (the anti-trust law) as well as from the official ideology of the United States, the land of free spirits, lone rangers, and entrepreneurs (Agassi 1985). In the decades that followed World War II, some residues from the Manhattan Project remained. For example, collaboration on big projects remains because of budgetary constraints, and some leading institutions of higher education behave more like a cartel than competitors.

We are repeatedly told that Big Science requires too much of an investment—in terms of both money and energy—for any individual or even for any single corporate body or university. It thus allegedly requires a new social and political setting, not to mention an appropriate economic setting. The disastrous aspect of this argument is that it was taken as self-evident. Ever since, science and technology are regularly spoken of in one breath, as if they are professionally welded and codependent but otherwise autonomous. In short, no matter how convenient, the term *technoscience* is itself problematic, for it must be constituted from a variety of perspectives and examined simultaneously from a variety of critical perspectives.

At least we should agree with those using the term *technoscience* that the two related activities associated with science and science-based technology remain relatively unproblematic in the following sense. We can always blame technology for the errors of scientists, we can always address our grievances to a definite party (technical organizations), and that party, in turn, can always shift its responsibility to the other (science in the abstract). This vicious cycle, of course, lets everyone off the hook (and endangers the very lives of us all), since the generators of this cycle are shrewd at knowingly evading public criticism in this privileged cycle of deceit (while the general public is not sufficiently well organized to block harmful actions). That is, the cycle's contours are such that they let any claim for responsibility glide effortlessly, and it is an effort to speak of social responsibility as if it were an extraneous factor in the production, dissemination, and consumption of science and technology.

Just as the conflation of the roles of scientists and of technicians is problematic in assigning responsibility, there is a problem concerning the examination of the standard roles of spiritual leaders from the ranks of science and religion. There are two standard views on the matter: the one alleges that science is certain knowledge, based on logic and empirical facts, whereas religion is unfounded belief, based on nothing more than superstition and awe; the other presents the two as separate but equal discourses, worldviews, and communities. A brief review of the vast literature on the history of science reveals that science is set up as the only responsible reaction to the dogmatism of religious leaders. Their (alleged or real) dogmatism is evident in their holding as sacred petrified texts. When the religious leaders retort that their rationalism, too, is a dogma, the scientific leadership responds by pointing out a sharp contrast between religious dogmatism and the openness of science. This, the holders of the first view maintain, is evident in the ongoing revolutions brought about by ever fresh scientific discoveries, by the controversies in which scientists regularly engage, their eventual resolutions, and the development of a critical attitude toward all scientific reports, no matter how humble or prestigious. While science is dynamic, critical, and open-minded in its pursuit of truth and therefore responsible through and through, religion (because it discovered the truth once and for all) is petrified, dogmatic, and closed-minded, and therefore cannot be held responsible for the social inadequacies of this or that regime.

I recite this whole debate to illustrate how academics can contribute to a cultural critique, rather than be its scribes. Their training and background knowledge make them especially fit to interject, suggest, and provide alternatives. They can be spokespeople, translators, and communicators. They can make accessible that which seems too esoteric for general comprehension. They can reduce the intimidation factor that enters public debates when scientists and intellectuals are at each other's intellectual throats. They can suggest here, for example, that some scientists are religious, some are not. They realize as well that to be scientifically committed to a certain (scientific) methodology does not mean to be completely committed to that methodology as a way of life; and finally, that the pursuit of truth is not limited to one community, be it scientifically minded or the religiously inclined.

In this respect, then, both scientific and religious communities rely on their group dynamics and the goodwill of their respective memberships, so that the different leaderships adopt similar modes of conduct. For example, both leaderships assert their authority and demand obedience and respect, and, oddly enough, in both cases it is respect based on knowledge proper and not on brute force. In addition, both leaderships recognize the power of faith and adhere to the machinations of faith healers, demanding awe, expecting adherence to strict pedagogical methods, delivering the "goods," and predicting the future. Finally, according to this view, both leaderships rely on tradition, paying homage to their respective spiritual ancestors, they expect the same respect to be granted to them in due course, and they hope that the future will grant them entry into the ranks of their illustrious progenitors.

Whether the similarity between the leaderships of religion and of science relies on the standards of faith healers or that of tradition makes no difference in our anticipation that both leaderships should assume responsibility for the actions and decisions undertaken within the academy. There are several problems with these two standard views of the interaction between science and religion (see, e.g., Barbour 1966). First, though we take it for granted that the intentions of scientists are honorable, the activities of practicing scientists turn out to be as institutionally corrupt as any others. Hence, they are not as averse as they should be to intellectual dogmatism in general and the closed-mindedness of their leaderships in particular. Second, it is not quite clear whether the contrast between science and religion stands to reason, for it is not clear what definitions of science and religion are used. That is, if a reductionist and ridiculing portrayal of religion is employed, then of course religion will pale by comparison to science. Likewise, a ridiculing portrayal of science would not match the convenient distinction previously described. Third, if we examine not only the canonical texts associated with science and religion in their respective histories but also their structure as communities of participants, then we find a much more complex view of their extracommunal relationships and their internal ideologies. By extension, there is a much more complex view concerning the responsibility assigned to scientific and religious leaderships during and after World War II.

The cultural setting that interests me here includes the academy. As far as the academy is concerned, I assume it could protect science form external pressures, preserve its structure and attainments from one generation to another, and transport its knowledge to any other subculture or society. Let us examine these alternative situations in turn and relate them all to the events of World War II.

First, consider the preservation of science as a community or as a culture. What is it that is preserved—shielded and protected—in the name of all that is dear to us as science? Is it a body of knowledge, such as a set of mathematical equations, or a set of reports on some empirical observations? Is it the specific products and results of scientific or technological research, or is it, by contrast, a general ethos—a way of thinking, an attitude toward the world and one's fellow inhabitants of this world? One historiographic view of the progress of science explains scientific progress and success in terms of the cumulative nature of science (Agassi 1963). According to this view, then, what is preserved, and thus what should be preserved within the academy, is the entire corpus of scientific knowledge with all of its details, as it has been accumulated ever since the ancient world, with more attention being paid to its latest products. Preservation in this sense means the recording of all relevant scientific knowledge and its study. Preservation here has not only a practical feature—how to preserve—but also a pedagogical feature—why to preserve. One may answer that this is for the sake of teaching students about science in order to make them better equipped to be scientists themselves or in order to have them respect science's successes almost religiously.

Second, with rationality and criticism as the bedrock of the university we can move, then, from one generation to another, from one historical contingency to another, preserving, as it were, an island of rationality and criticism. This sort of reconstructed narrative sounds appealing in the German context, thus leading us from the texts of Sir Francis Bacon and René Descartes through those of Immanuel Kant and G. W. F. Hegel, to those of Friedrich Nietzsche and Edmund Husserl, and thus right into World War II. All of these thinkers, whether representatives or critics of their culture, retained a deep sense of respect toward science. Even the romantic reaction to science took it for granted that science was an important cultural phenomenon that couldn't and shouldn't be ignored, no matter how narrow-minded are its bearers and no matter how inadequate it may turn out to be as a means for personal redemption (Cohen and Wartofsky 1984). Within their national borders, cultures could ignore science no more than they could ignore religious institutions, like the Roman Catholic Church. Though these institutions annoyingly demanded political independence, states supported financially and ideologically the conduct of religion and science alike, though separately (Amrine, Zucker, and Wheeler 1987).

Third, the transfer of the products of science in the university setting from one culture to another is clearly perceived if one holds on to the principles of rationality and criticism, the need to ground science in logic and in empirical testing. Not only is the perception of the preservation of these principles readily available, there is a rationale for the perception, an attendant explanation that supports the expectation that science can indeed be preserved regardless of cultural or national boundaries, which is precisely how it can transcend them. The perception and explanation of this situation is termed *universalism*. The rules of logic, for instance, should hold regardless of what language one uses or the diet to which one is accustomed. The logical distinction between a proposition and its negation holds true for any person in the world, no matter what particular proposition is examined and no matter how negation is expressed in the local dialect. A logical inconsistency can be discerned no matter in what linguistic apparatus we examine it. And, likewise, an empirical observation can be shared by people around the globe, no matter in what language they report their observations.

This universalist orientation contained a promise no one could reject, namely, the prospect for world peace (or perpetual peace, as Kant envisioned it). For a world engulfed in incessant battles and long-lasting wars, the prospect of world peace was sufficient ground to adopt a universalist cultural stance in the name of science or supported by the scientific discourse. In this context, all disputes are in principle rapidly resolvable, because they are all the result of either flawed logical operations or poor observations of the facts. Both errors are relatively rapidly correctable, again, in principle, and therefore the promise for the future is immensely powerful and appealing.

AVOIDING THE ERRORS OF
UNIVERSALISM AND NATIONALISM

If universalism were solely equated with utopianism, my exposition here concerning the preservation of science in the academy would have been quite simple. I could illustrate the great advantages of universalism, such as world peace, use them heuristically, and attempt to structure a future university that would rest on universalist attitudes and avoid the atrocities of Auschwitz and Hiroshima. But universalism is an absolutist view whose transcendence of all historical and national limits overlooks the significance of historical contingencies and the peculiarities, economic and others, of local communities.

Perhaps there is yet another way of putting the matter: an insistence on universalism ignores the inapplicability, not to mention the dangerous dogmatism, of universalism in various contexts (which is inherent in its very refusal to recognize any specific context, of course). Universalists reject these charges; they declare the ill effects of the application of universalism's misapplications, the unjust hiding behind grand principles, and they declare that, like physics, universalism applies the universal law to specific contexts to obtain specific recommendations. Yet this is precisely where the error of the universalists lies: they have never presented a social theory as all-embracing as the law of gravity. And in the absence of such a law, one can never know what characteristics of a specific situation pertain to the specifications of the prescriptions for improvement. Attempts to implement universalism thus land in chaos out of ignorance of what is to be prescribed. When these attempts fail, the adherents of universalism, who equate it with reason, ascribe the failure to the refusal of the populace to accept the precepts of reason, thus shifting the responsibility from the manufacturers of scientific technology to the unsuspecting public.

Universalists then may and usually do resort to the use of force. Hence, universalism can easily deteriorate into intellectual tyranny. Plato, for example, suggested that the knowledge of the laws of heredity should govern matchmaking, under government tutelage, of course. By now we obviously expect that there is no room for (allegedly or truly) scientific intervention in matters of the heart. For example, that we tell students that Yankee ingenuity has been the touchstone of U.S. capitalism is one thing; but this does not justify the hatred for foreigners and the resistance to immigration. The slippage of universalism to nationalism overlooks the obvious historical record of the last two centuries, which shows clearly that the ingenuity of immigrants has borne so many things American, of which the nationalists are so proud. Are these immigrants nationalist themselves, once they are permitted to become U.S. citizens? Do they exemplify a national ethos, or are they by definition defying national boundaries since they have come from around the world? And is the ethos of patriotism a cover for latent nationalism?

Patriotism is an important cultural phenomenon in relation to science for three reasons. First, romantic nationalism is understood historically to have been a reaction to Enlightenment universalism. Hence, to reject universalism or find its errors (of absolutist narrow-mindedness) may seem at first an inducement to adopt nationalism. But this will not do, since nationalism can turn out to be, as in the extreme case of German National Socialism, just as fanatical, rigid, absolutist, and tyrannical in the extreme.

Second, the ideology of nationalism may dictate the interaction of the scientific community and the culture in which it operates. In some extreme cases, as in the former Soviet Union, it meant proposing proletariat science to replace bourgeois science as if the former is objective while the latter biased. In Nazi Germany it meant the rejection of all scientific theories associated with Jews so as to favor only Aryan ones, whatever they may be. In this respect, then, the influence and pressure by state ideology in the name of nationalism may undermine irresponsibly (here, in a social and political sense, not only in a methodological sense) the two principles of rationality and criticism mentioned previously.

And third, it is possible that nationalist attitude will influence the internal working of the scientific community. The social dynamics of the scientific community and its leadership—as Michael Polanyi (1969) and Thomas Kuhn (1970) both stress—harbor prejudices that influence the production of scientific discoveries and technological innovations.

Nationalism, in a manner different from patriotism and universalism, may turn out to be a strong ideological vehicle through which to convince scientists that their work is significant for their country. It could be construed as a means to save and help their fellow citizens and as a means to ensure not only their own survival and that of their fellow citizens but also to defeat their enemies so that no threat will ever impede their national aspirations and their freedom. The rhetoric with which the appeal is made, as noted already in the case of the Manhattan Project, is such that individual scientists find themselves in the following quandary. Either I participate and cooperate and save my country but also produce nuclear weapons that will kill millions, or I refuse to participate and thereby allow the killings of my fellow citizens by an aggressive enemy. One way out of this quandary in the nineteenth century for the majority of German scientists was to declare themselves universalists in scientific matters and nationalists in politics. But this, of course, will not do. History shows that in such cases universal science serves the worst dictates or irresponsible national leaders. This kind of quandary already appears in Henrik Ibsen's *An Enemy of the People* (1882), where the village doctor is supposed to rely on the findings of scientific technology (the laboratory testing of water samples) in order to determine scientifically whether or not it is hazardous for the public to use the recently developed local baths. The dilemma or quandary in this case seems relatively minor compared with that of Nazi doctors, since the worst that can happen in Ibsen's case is the financial ruin of a village. By contrast, in the case of Nazi Germany thousands of prisoners in concentration camps were subjected to lethal and fatal experiments.

What Ibsen's doctor exemplifies, though, is the intervention of political leaders on behalf of local interest that may conflict with the universalist pretensions of the scientific community. In whose name is the doctor speaking? Whose interests ought to be regarded first and foremost and therefore protected jealously? Is there a way to satisfy both universal and local demands simultaneously? These questions, as Bernard Shaw so aptly portrays them (1906), remain part and parcel of the daily workings of the scientific community, no matter the composition of its ranks and no matter where it operates, that is, no matter what national stigma is attached to it (Laor and Agassi 1990).

At this juncture, of course, critical intellectuals in the academy, isolated from the public debate, are entrusted not to reveal the quandary to anyone because it is both an academic (an esoteric) secret and a secret of the universalist movement. There has to be a way to remain patriotic—love oneself and one's tradition—without thereby surrendering all faculties of judgment. But how can this be accomplished in a responsible manner? Will an appeal to academics as critical thinkers save the day? Are academics father- and mother-confessors to whom one may appeal, who might hopefully free scientists from their burden and ensure that they can return to their laboratories unharmed?

Perhaps all they have to do, as Bertrand Russell (1950) suggested, is study some philosophy and be redeemed. Perhaps Russell's suggestion does not go far enough: all frustrated and confused scientists should quit their jobs as scientists and become philosophers of science instead; all intellectuals should be critical enough to offer political alternatives and teach their students to worry about their eventual social positions. Still, even when enough job training is done to convert students to their philosophical posts, the activities we associate with science and technology will continue. Moreover, what will the professors teach students and the public that they do not already know?

Between the two alternatives of universalism and nationalism, between an appeal to the entire world and an appeal to ignore the entire world, there must be another alternative. This alternative should not be one that pretends to subsume one alternative into another, as Hegel tried to include the universalism of a world spirit into his nationalist commitments (viewing Napoleon as the world spirit on a white horse). This sort of an attempt is misleading in its claim to endorse both alternatives and bring them together. What seems at first an uncritical acceptance of both of them as they are turns out to be a feigned acceptance of universalism and a committed endorsement of nationalism. The result of this combination is a radical and extreme nationalism under the guise of classical cosmopolitanism that was allegedly a worldwide nationalism.

PLURALISM IN THE NEXT CENTURY

I propose to reconsider the alluring promise of world peace offered by enlightened and humane pluralism, a pluralism that preserves science as a version of critical rationality within culture, no matter how idealistic this may sound. The academy, in light of its medieval past, could prove to be a sanctuary where pluralism is celebrated albeit critically.

Consider the case of Pierre Duhem, a physicist, philosopher, and historian of science, one of the giants in the intellectual world of the turn of the century, and the tome of the notorious Dreyfus Affair. He was a broad-minded, culturally tuned scholar, and a narrow-minded chauvinist. His historically informed philosophical reflections on science distinguish between the German and the French scientific mind, claiming that while the French have an imaginative and creative mind, the German excel in their attention to details, logical and others. It is from this nationalist perspective that he tried to explain the difference between German and French science, with the obvious expectations notwithstanding, in terms of national traits. Duhem's conclusions are not limited to pedagogical techniques employed differently in the two countries and therefore influencing students in certain forms. Instead, his insistence is more fundamental, claiming these national traits to be ingrained, natural phenomena (Duhem 1990).

That Duhem's view is erroneous goes without saying. But what is much more alarming is the fact that the revered Duhem propounded views not much different from those of Francis Galton (1869) concerning eugenics. Galton was at the time a famous biologist, geologist, anthropologist, philosopher, and a member of the scientific leadership in England in the second half of the nineteenth century (and a cousin of Charles Darwin). Galton's eugenics was presented to the scientific world as an established fact, and he organized the now infamous but then highly respectable Eugenic Society, which aimed at implementing responsibly—whatever this meant—the practical aspects of his eugenic findings.

The incredible fact is that the ideas of Galton (and by implication even some of Duhem's) were first considered scientific and then found their way, directly or indirectly, to the ideas of Nazi ideologues who made their claims about national traits—killing millions in the name of pure race. They based their murders on so-called biological, hence scientific, theories and principles that were only later accepted as a mere facade of statistical respectability for an ideological stance a priori abhorred by most critical people. However, Galton's example illustrates my concern with the responsibility of individual professors.

Moreover, his example reminds us how easy it is to distinguish between the academy as a perfect sanctuary and individual professors as humans who are fallible. The focus on professors as a community of critics, with a code of internal rules of conduct and a full-fledged hierarchy, is no shift from an ideal academy, but indeed a recognition that the very foundation of the academy is intimately connected with those who "make," produce, and disseminate knowledge. Its consumers, of course, are normally secondary in the minds of many academics (because they think they write only for their fellow-academics), and there is where some of the public puzzle over the role and responsibility of professors comes from.

As I have suggested elsewhere (Sassower 1998), the discourse on these questions imposes on its participants a discussion about the nature of science, which is better avoided here. So it is much better—intellectually preferable and more responsible and more politically oriented—to ask instead: what safeguards must be established in order to ensure that Auschwitz and Hiroshima will not happen again?

This, then, is clear: the solution is neither the universalism of science nor the nationalism of the states with which the members of the academic community are of necessity affiliated. Can the academy police itself as is expected of the scientific community (see more on this in Hoekema 1994 and Markie 1994)? Is the option of a self-policing scientific community serious? Michael Polanyi (1969) recommended this, and Karl Popper (1972) recommended self-censorship of the individual researcher. Yet no scientific tribunal ever evaluated its self-policing procedures and results. Instead the scientific community always assumes that they are in place and therefore require no scrutiny. A similar description would fit the university system in general. The sanctuary of the academy insulates individual professors from the kind of accountability corporate leaders must confront (as explained in Weingartner 1999).

In a perverse sense, C. P. Snow, in his famous little pamphlet on the so-called two cultures (1964), endorses the universalism of science in the face of other intellectual pursuits—those of literature, poetry, and the arts. But his version of that universalism is such that it separates science from its intellectual surroundings, divorces it from its cultural milieu, so that scientists can talk only to other scientists but to no one else. Of course it is wonderful if scientists from different countries can communicate with each other, but as long as their communication is limited to the technical matters of their research, society cannot benefit enough from their communication. As we saw in the case of Nazi scientists, they inevitably communicated with their culture and thereby yielded to politicians and scientific leaders who funded them and expected certain results from their socially sanctioned investment. Snow speaks of the ethos of science as "future-oriented," and this indeed is the self-image of the Enlightenment researcher; but the same "future-oriented" scientists, Snow knows, serve their governments and their own interests shamelessly in the present.

Snow's view, no less than Duhem's, is erroneous and dangerous at the same time. Unintentionally, perhaps, his view implies that Nazi scientists, just like their U.S. counterparts, could claim allegiance to abstract universalist scientific principles, while ignoring the atrocities in which they actively participated while contributing to the war effort of their country. They could worship their mathematical tools and techniques, while dismissing the context in which they were executed. As scientists, Snow implies, they could never be found guilty of anything, since all they did was the work of science. If anyone was at fault, it was the technicians who installed the gases in concentration camps according to military orders that were followed because of political policies. By this scenario scientists remain hidden from the public eye, merely experts in the ivory tower, the island of learning, far away from the realities of daily life and from the commonsense that is required for daily survival (Sassower 1993).

Perhaps I should stress in this context that my concern remains with the justification of the maintenance of the welfare system of the academy or higher education, a system that could benefit our culture just as much as (if not more than) the military welfare system. My concern remains with the critical dimension that could be added in the preparation of future generations for their ability to survive and progress over time and improve the lot of the citizens without losing sight of the community as a whole. The fragile balance between individual rights and aspirations and the needs of the community is difficult to observe and keep alive. This is a balance I have described in the previous two chapters and one that I will return to in subsequent chapters. This balance, incidentally, is not limited to the role of intellectuals and the institutions of higher education where they work; rather, it is a balance we need to appreciate if we want to understand the context within which this balance is maintained.

I am not speaking here of democratic societies in some general sense, but instead about the particular procedures that constitute a democracy and that ought to be perpetuated and upheld by intellectuals. To be more specific, intellectuals as cultural critics should take a leading, and therefore responsible, role in democratizing their respective societies. Instead of either endorsing or rejecting a state ideology or the ideology of the so-called stateless scientific community, cultural critics should first and foremost explore the roots of all ideologies and do so critically. They should propose alternatives to these ideologies and repeatedly explore the practical consequences that ensue from upholding these ideological commitments fervently. The issue is not that ideologies may turn out to be erroneous; we all agree that by definition this is the case. Rather, the issue is the absolutist endorsement of ideologies and their uncritical application; and this is a matter of responsibility, both intellectual and moral, especially in the aftermath of the terrible events of World War II.

4

+

Academic Confusions

CONNECTIONS

In chapter 3 I tried to connect ethical questions about the behavior and thought processes of academics within the emerging model with the responsibility that should be felt by the technoscientific community. In this chapter I examine the paradoxical position academics must accept when attempting to bridge intellectual gaps in education while protecting and preserving their own fields of expertise. Academics are confused not only about their split loyalty between teaching and research and between their students and themselves but also about the more general role the university must play in this century. Are academics servants of their cultural settings, providing social goods for their sponsors and the general public? Are they, instead, independent scholars who found sanctuary behind university walls? The changes of the emerging model of higher education may turn these two questions on their heads and require us to pose different questions and definitely provide different answers. Since the model may no longer be about research and teaching, the imparting of knowledge, or the improvement of the mind, our culture might therefore be telling us a story we must listen to if not approve.

The story I have been hearing for the past two decades is a story about professionalism, making money, and using the academy for the improvement of one's financial position in life. If this is the case, my own plea for the life of the mind, for the love of studying seemingly useless knowledge (Graber 1995), even for what may be seen as waste (chapter 1) all will turn out to be important issues we should critically examine. Incidentally, my appeal here is for critical engagement, but not the fluffy one of those who are too lazy to read and think but enjoy solving simple logical puzzles. Rather, my appeal will work only if we are all ready to work hard on exercising our minds.

Someone could suggest that my appeal for the improvement of the life of the mind might be a throwback to the past, a conservative move, even a reactionary one, as they call it. This is not a conservative cry for standards and basic (foundational) knowledge; rather, it is a warning sign that sometimes in the name of interdisciplinary studies, whole fields of research might be eliminated. And at other times, in the name of professionalizing knowledge, whole traditions of critical thinking can be lost. For example, we forget that it might be more effective to teach computer science students the history of computer languages rather than yet another specific computer language. This way students would appreciate the dead ends of the past and the reasons for innovative new steps, instead of just figuring out the details of this or that language. Once again, my way of thinking about knowledge acquisition is not a way to hold on to old truths. Rather it is a way to appreciate the nuances of why some puzzles cannot be solved the old way and why new ways must be introduced. So, however impractical it seems to study the anachronistic past, it is the development of that past into the present that sheds light on what might be useful in the future.

I will explain what I'm concerned with here by relating it to medical education, for two reasons. The first has to do with the awe we have for medical miracles and the prestige associated with doctors. The second has to do with medicine as a field of inquiry and practice that is both a science and an art, though from the prestige perspective it is the scientific element that is commonly lauded by the media and the public. If I can convince you how medical education should be changed, then you might more readily agree that all higher (and even professional) education should be changed. The goal, in my mind, would be to improve both the life of students as intellectuals in the making, and through this, improve the lot of those who come in contact with them either as consumers, clients, or friends. But before we get to medical schools, let's spend a couple of extra pages reviewing the context of the university system that has evolved over the past one-half century. What makes it interesting is the fact that after World War II there has been an economic boom that has prompted additional expenditure on education, notwithstanding the GI Bill. But the university no longer stood as a citadel of higher learning and esoteric scholarship. Instead, it became more involved, as we saw in chapter 3, with research and development of so-called Big Science: projects that require thousands of researchers coordinating their efforts to solve technical problems and come up with scientific discoveries and their application.

THE MULTIVERSITY

Clark Kerr's notion of the 1960s "multiversity," the model for the new configuration of higher education, is the following. "A university anywhere can aim no higher than to be as British as possible for the sake of the undergraduates, as German as possible for the sake of the graduates and the research personnel, as American as possible for the sake of the public at large—and as confused as possible for the sake of the preservation of the whole uneasy balance" (1963, 18). Following Fritz Machlup's concern with "knowledge production" and the significance of this economic phenomenon in the second half of the twentieth century (1962), Kerr explains what he perceives to be the importance of the production of knowledge in the university system: "Knowledge has certainly never in history been so central to the conduct of an entire society. What the railroads did for the second half of the last century and the automobile for the first half of this century may be done for the second half of this century by the knowledge industry: that is, to serve as the focal point for national growth. And the university is at the center of the knowledge process" (1963, 88). It is possible to extrapolate from Kerr's notion of the knowledge industry that even if it were limited to specific modes of data gathering and dissemination, it should be pliable enough to appeal to a variety of consumers. This means that when potential consumers cannot be consulted ahead of time to modify modes of delivery of knowledge claims, the producers have to anticipate their customers' preferences and allow for later revisions and restructuring. How will they accomplish this task? By using art and imagination, envisioning what might be liked or disliked, found useful or useless (for more on this, see Sassower 1995, 133–40). The knowledge industry, then, is an industry the demands on which are no different from those that produce other goods and services, since one cannot assume that supply will bring about its own demand.

In my view, all students, however ill prepared, should be invited into the multiversity. They can find different tracks adjustable to their needs, interests, qualification, and aspirations. They can stay as long as they wish or leave at any time. They should be participants in determining the direction the academy takes, while acknowledging their dependence on their instructors, those whose prior knowledge and experience privileges them temporarily and for particular purposes under specific circumstances. Perhaps there is a way to break down some of the negative medieval features of the university as it transforms itself into a multiversity. Perhaps it can overthrow its indebtedness to the church and to its own hierarchical structure. Perhaps it can retain some of the features that made the university a threat to both church and state, namely, its claim for independence. In short, perhaps the multiversity can become a cultural powerhouse that contributes to its surroundings while maintaining a critical distance.

As I described earlier in this book, intellectuals are confused about their status as refugees in a sanctuary and as public servants living by the grace of the state or private patrons. Their confusion is about what is expected of them outside of what they themselves expect of themselves. So, no matter how many codes are adopted at the university, and no matter how many panels are assembled to review the conduct of academics, they will always remain ambivalent about their position in society. Therefore, I plead for something other than adhering to yet another code of conduct. I appeal to the common-sense appreciation of why we should support a sanctuary of their and our own. This would be a place where ideas are circulated, where the intellectual appetite is wetted all the time, where curiosity is applauded as opposed to ridiculed, and where creativity can mean almost anything from experiment in organic chemistry to on-stage performances.

Back to the multiversity. If the multiversity is characterized by the knowledge industry, and if the knowledge industry as an industry is driven by so-called market forces, then is there room for anyone's creativity? Only if we maintain the notion of a sanctuary can creativity be promoted. When we are supposed to produce creative works under the gun, so to speak, the results may be less than satisfactory. We can only look back to totalitarian regimes, like Nazi Germany and communist Soviet Union, to see the disastrous results of such imposition of power. Those of you who will counter with wonderful examples from that era must admit that you are bringing up the names of refugees and dissidents and not those paid by the government to be mouthpieces for its ideological tenets.

THE PRACTICE OF MEDICAL DISCOURSE

S. Poirier and D. J. Brauner have argued that "there is a need in current medical genres to introduce a language that will do . . . as little *violence* as possible to the *presence* of both patient and physician" (1988, 9). In order to deliver what they consider "optimal health care," the authors identify a synthesis between the scientific and the human for (what they perceive as) a true understanding to take place between patients and physicians. Such a synthesis is inspired by the works of Jacques Derrida, whose terminology is used extensively in their article.

However, if one adopts the philosophical framework of Derrida's works, it seems that Poirier and Brauner have appropriated only partial aspects of his philosophical ideas. It is true that a "narrative" in Derrida's sense must "provide the opportunity to integrate a patient's social history with the other sections of his or her story" so as "to encourage a holistic approach to patient care" (Poirier and Brauner 1988, 6). But when saying this, two related issues come to mind, and not only the one the authors emphasize. First, is holistic medicine more "effective" than "mainstream" medicine? If yes, how and to what extent? Second, is it possible to have any "story" or "narrative" that is "accurate" or accurately represents the medical status of patients? Both of these questions are lumped inadvertently into one issue, an important issue of the communication that ought to take place between physicians and patients in order to increase the potential for successful treatment.

In what follows, I want to argue that there needs to be a shift in emphasis (and not a full paradigm shift in the Kuhnian sense) concerning the relationship between patients and physicians. This shift involves two stages. First, the focus must be turned away from the patient–physician interaction and communication, since such focus comes at the end of a long process through which physicians receive their education and training, in short, their medical worldview(s). Second, after there has been enough focused attention on the process of medical indoctrination and initiation, there would be good reason to return to the examination of patient–physician relationship. Under these circumstances, this examination would be done with a different mode of thinking, such that issues of autonomy and paternalism are not necessarily linked to patients and physicians respectively.

This two-stage approach to the provision of health care is based on the following hypothesis: ethical dilemmas arising in and through the interaction of physicians and patients are a result of an unwarranted and misguided medical training process. If the hypothesis is refuted, showing, for example, that changes in the education of physicians does not eliminate ethical problems associated with "inappropriate attitudes" of physicians (e.g., paternalism), revising medical education can still lead to a change in public orientation toward the medical profession.

This hypothesis is similar but not identical to the following hypothesis: ethical dilemmas arising in and through the interaction of physicians and patients are a result of an unwarranted and misguided view of the scientific foundation of medicine. The focus in medical training is based to a large extent on the widely held assumption that such training is linked to the scientific model(s) of medicine without accounting for the "nonepistemic character" of medicine and its implications on the study and practice of medicine (Engelhardt 1986, 177–8).

The hypothesis about medical training leads to the following prediction: if the hypothesis is corroborated and not refuted (i.e., maintaining a sense of tentative truth value), we will eliminate most of the dilemmas that arise when patients encounter physicians. The practical suggestions that follow attempt to address this prediction so as to set the stage for the revision of medical training.

It seems that articles similar to the one cited previously would turn out to be of little value, since they attempt to "solve" ethical problems after the fact instead of providing the means by which to prevent them from arising in the first place. Put differently, the discussion of "miscommunication" concerning the intimacy and immediacy of relations between patients and physicians is secondary to the roles both parties believe they play in light of their respective perceived backgrounds. This comes close to what Jay Katz says in *The Silent World of Doctor and Patient* (1984), but it seems that Katz does not say enough. The most relevant aspects of his book that deal with medical education are discussed later.

In order to examine medical education, the training of physicians for their roles as health care providers, one must mention the presuppositions that underlie such an education. The literature on the language(s) of medicine and the literature about the importance of these languages to medical practice are by now common knowledge. Specific events, such as the spread of AIDS, encourage a restatement of the metaphors we use to describe "disease," "illness," or "well-being," as a means to understand the cultural matrix within which these metaphors take hold (cf., Sontag 1977 and 1988). And the philosophical literature on the ways in which medicine has historically appropriated reality and redefined it in its own manner for its own purposes is also extensive and illuminating (cf., Fleck 1979 and Reznek 1987).

In light of this, then, the question is no longer whether or not the unique language of medicine differs from ordinary language or whether or not the medical "language game" (in Wittgenstein's sense) differs from other language games. Instead, the question has been set in the following terms: Does the difference in linguistic games set up barriers so that the effectiveness of health care provision is undermined? But even this question seems to have been answered in the affirmative quite readily in the past two decades (cf., Robins and Wolf 1988, 217–21). So, as my hypothesis proposes, maybe it is time to ask questions about the ethics of medical training and not merely restate the obvious, namely, that medical training overly emphasizes the scientific model (however poorly defined) and thereby leads to misconceptions and miscommunication that result in moral ambiguities and problems.

QUESTIONABLE FOUNDATIONS
FOR MEDICAL DISCOURSE

When approaching the question of medical education historically, there seem to be some provisional guidelines already in the Platonic dialogues. In Plato's *Republic*, we are told that medicine is both an art and a science and that "no science studies or enforces the interest of the controlling or stronger party, but rather that of the weaker party subjected to it" (342d). Even if Socrates ignores the "artistic" aspects of medicine, the sense of creative conjectures, of experimental open-endedness that artistic muses may encourage, his view of science seems pertinent, as Rudolph Napodano agrees, to the question of medical training (1986, 19–21). Medical practice is geared, in the Platonic worldview, toward the weaker, the patient, and is not for the sake of "profit," as he later says of the doctor's mission. A similar attitude toward the medical profession has become the standard cultural staple of modernity, with or without the specific principles of the Hippocratic oath.

Plato speaks of the science of medicine requiring the attention and care of the weaker party, and Jay Katz echoes Plato's concern with the practice of "medicine's art." They both emphasize the human side of medicine, the priority to be given to healing and caring for patients. More specifically, Katz believes that "to 'humanize' doctors" will require, some two thousand years after Plato's original statements, "'humanizing' their training" (1984, xx). One way in which to accomplish this task, according to Katz, is by teaching doctors how to converse with patients (1984, 152–3). Katz argues that the psychoanalytic process of transference and countertransference could help patients and physicians realize the similar reactions they have to certain culturally shared values and ideas and the extent to which they can all benefit when exchanging their ideas, feelings, and medical data. In short, some psychoanalytic techniques and some communication skills could go a long way toward improving the practice of physicians. However, these techniques and skills should not be at the expense of the regular technical scientific training that physicians undergo in medical school; they should supplement what is considered the standard scientific training.

The ultimate goal of the revision in medical training as far as Katz is concerned has to do with a change in decision-making processes, where patients become partners and not mere recipients of physicians' verdicts (1984, 228–9). The challenge to the traditional paternalistic role of physicians in terms of decision making, diagnosing patients, prescribing treatment, and predicting prognosis is based to a great extent on the realization that there are inherent uncertainties in medicine—understood here as a science and not as an art (1984, 204–5 and Sassower and Grodin 1987). But even Katz's concern with education— the scientific versus the humanistic training of physicians in medical schools—does not go far enough.

There is no question that certain scientific models have dominated medical training. In some cases this is good, for example, when the experimental method allows one to correlate certain "cause-and-effect" situations so that certain symptoms can be traced back to certain bacteria. In addition, the collective historical record of all patients ever treated anywhere in the world (something modern computer technology will make available in the near future) can serve as an excellent guide toward the diagnosis and prognosis of present and future patients. The power of these methods of probabilistic induction must remain uncontestable, regardless of the obvious fact that knowing a certain rate of probability does not ensure an accurate prediction of a specific case. As Napodano argues in line with the standard clinical perception of medical provision, "the traditional basic and clinical sciences and skills are the *bedrock* of a curriculum for the preparation of a physician" (1986, 88, emphasis added).

But this so-called bedrock of scientific models—inductive or deductive—has been under attack for a long time now. The debates that took place between the members of the Vienna Circle and Karl Popper during the period between the two world wars are still echoed today in academic circles. Thomas Kuhn's innovative suggestions about paradigm shifts, inspired by Ludwig Fleck's work on paradigm shifts in medicine, and the social dynamics of the scientific community lead one to suspect the scientific validity and truth of knowledge claims. And the crusade against any canonical scientific methodology by Paul Feyerabend suggests that even if we can't take the position that "anything goes," a great latitude and tolerance ought to be shown to allegedly nontraditional or nonscientific (or pseudoscientific, from the perspective of Western medicine) practices such as Chinese medicine and tribal herbal medicine. The political aspects of the scientific community, open to personal rivalry and power plays, have been exposed historically by sociologists, such as Robert Merton, and philosophers, such as Joseph Agassi. So, what does this accumulated information reveal about the training of physicians?

In light of this, Katz's answer is insufficient, for he wishes to supplement the given rather than challenge it. Besides, what is "given" to students, the tradition that is "handed down" from one generation of practitioners and educators to the next, is not only a story in Derrida's sense but also a myth and disguise. Napodano's answer is insufficient as well. Though he agrees that "the preparation and educational development of a person for a career in the practice of the profession of medicine ought to be founded upon a comprehensive knowledge base" that includes "values and virtues" (1986, 12, 16–18), he still confines his suggestions to the creation of a "balance between science and compassion" (1986, 65). In this respect, he too remains committed to some standards of scientific knowledge and competence that remain open to fundamental challenges.

Only if one accepts all knowledge to be mythical, or a story, only when one recognizes that there is no difference between myths, stories, narratives, legends, and legacies, then one can welcome the suggestions that follow here (cf., Ormiston and Sassower 1989). That is to say, only when one is prepared to question all presuppositions that underlie medical education and training—linguistic, epistemological, and even metaphysical—then one can undertake to revise the curriculum.

THE ETHICAL DIMENSION
OF MEDICAL TRAINING

My suggestions regarding the revamping of medical education are linked to my view that the contemporary focus of medical ethics is misplaced. Physicians, and not patients, are the ones who are set up to be at an ethically disadvantaged position. It is not only the patient who is ignorant, depending on the "expert" advice of the physician, who is thus ushered into the problems of autonomy, paternalism, and the like. Instead, it is the physicians who also suffer from "ignorance," since they are led to believe that there is such a thing as "medical expertise." Moreover, they believe that medical knowledge is based on "science" and not on the accumulated knowledge of past experiences and that some "stories" are more accurate and more appropriate than others. In short, they are taught that medicine is not a communal effort, but the heroic effort of a few experts. Using the word *story* to describe not only fairy tales and novels but any discourse that attempts to provide a systematic "presentation" of a given situation from a particular perspective, I adopt here the contemporary so-called deconstructivist or postmodern terminology.

From what has been just said one can conclude that in attacking the scientific model of medical expertise and, hence, physician training based on that model, what is offered here is in fact an alternate model or story. But if no story is in principle preferable to any other, how is the present story distinguishable or more convincing than any other? From one perspective, at issue is not a mere preference of one story or model over another, but the presentation of "my" model or story in addition to others. That is, medical training would change radically not only if one model were to be replaced with another but also if such replacement does not occur but instead there is an introduction of additional models to the ones currently presented. It seemed that the very introduction of alternative models and stories may change the fundamental commitment to the exclusivity (and validity) of a single scientific model.

From another perspective, it may not be a question of which story is more accurate than all others but which one fits better or is more appropriate for a specific goal. When one has a choice between alternatives, it becomes more palatable than before to think in terms of practical usage to which one model is better suited than another. This is not the same as choosing once and for all—as an undergraduate or a medical student—the scientific model as the only model that fits medicine. On the contrary, the choice one makes between competing models remains flexible without being careless about which particular technique based on a specific model is to be used in this case as opposed to a different case.

To some extent the pragmatic thrust of my orientation is quite common especially within the American tradition. However, medical students are indoctrinated to believe that the medical community is a scientific community and that scientific communities operate unlike neighborhood communities or the communities of poets (cf., Feyerabend 1978 and Agassi 1981). Our privileging the medical community and ascribing to it a unique mode of thinking and behavior puts physicians in a confused and confusing intellectual as well as moral position.

In this respect, then, medical students are robbed of their cultural heritage while being required to answer the pragmatic demands and changing whims of the same culture. They are offered the protection of science, although science itself has found no protection of late from the attack of anyone who wishes to engage in scientific discourse—no matter how that discourse is defined or interpreted. This confusion can be detected in the proliferation of "how-to" coping manuals that are designed for incoming medical students (cf., Virshup 1985).

Furthermore, medical students are promised and even guaranteed some moral superiority in advance because they will be the healers and (physical) savers of society, while at the same time being continuously reminded that the notions of healing, treating, and curing are all open to criticism. As J. Bynum and G. Sheets argue, a change in students' attitudes "represents a subtle coping or defense mechanism . . . response to the trauma of daily confrontations with human suffering" (1985, 182).

And finally, there is the problem of the change in personal characteristics—even personality change—especially in terms of stress, that students undergo between the time they are accepted into medical schools and the time they graduate with licenses to practice medicine, a period that can be as long as eight to ten years, depending on specialties (McFall 1986). Students might have had one set of motivations to pursue this course of study, but once confronted with a certain mystique surrounding their particular role as health care providers, they might be transformed and feel a different sense of empowerment. For example, one study that attempted to figure out the changes in sociopolitical attitudes notes a shift toward conservative perspective by the end of medical training. But it is not definite whether such a shift is solely attributable to medical training or is also a result of maturation (Maheux and Beland 1987).

To a great extent, those who can use some compassion and moral support are not only patients—who by now demand these things in court—but physicians. If any change is possible, it must be at the very beginning of medical training, even before students enter the halls of medical schools. The State of New York forbids interns to sleep too little as part of their training (unfortunately because of accidents and not because such training is deemed inhuman). It is also time that the deans of all medical schools require students to "lose sleep" over their emotional and psychological propensities and dispositions instead of over the inability to memorize yet another Latin term in physiology.

The focus on students' psychological propensities and dispositions are especially pertinent in the case of medical students who must have had excellent grades and test scores in order to be able to enter medical schools in the first place. Such highly motivated and driven individuals, who have had to compete hard to obtain their entrance certificate, have to learn how to "change gears," how to appreciate their medical training in cooperative and collaborative terms and no longer in competitive terms alone. This is not to say that competition should not be part of medical education, only that it should not hamper the emotional and psychological growth that physicians must accomplish before they are fit to enter their official roles.

As James Knight suggests, the medical school environment has much to do with the success or failure of medical students. For some the competitive environment is so harmful that they may need to quit altogether (1973, 47–8). For others the administrative structure and educational atmosphere are so daunting, especially in view of the scientific role model of the professors, that students end up confused about how they should adopt and adapt their own personality traits to fit the medical scientific mold (Knight, 81–3). Knight follows Koestler's discussion of the three "character types in science" that include the Benevolent Magician, the Mad Professor, and the Uninspired Pedant.

Instead of having undergraduate premedical programs that emphasize the acquaintance and mastery of the sciences, there should be a premedical program that questions the inclination of students to become health care professionals and thus caters to what Knight calls "psychologic maturation" (1973, 46–7). The study of the history of medicine, the philosophy of medicine, and the sociology of medicine should be a prerequisite for an acceptance to medical schools. Students should be expected to have had several courses in psychology, not only experimental or behavioral psychology. They should take several sociology courses so that they understand the cultural diversity of the patient population with which they will eventually interact. They should take history courses not only related to medicine but related to the country in which medical practice is so highly valued in monetary terms and in terms of social status. They should take courses in philosophy and theology to determine what view of human nature they are inclined to adopt, what view of the relation between human beings they find most persuasive (e.g., competitive versus cooperative), and what view of themselves they have. And finally, students should take enough communication courses so they can appreciate the strengths and deficiencies of their own communication skills.

Even if a heavier dose of humanities courses at the undergraduate level does not do away with ethical dilemmas, it might help medical students and physicians cope with such dilemmas. In other words, ethical dilemmas will always appear in health-care provision, but instead of being startled and forced into making quick decisions they might eventually regret or that might be found unacceptable by others, physicians will be prepared to deal with dilemmas and to diffuse potential tense relations with their patients. Knowing, for example, that a conflict of authority (who should decide what to do?) could arise in a certain situation—a living will for a terminally ill patient, for instance—will alert physicians to approach the situation in a way that is neither paternalistic nor manipulative but in a way that involves the patient or the patient's family in deciding on either a certain procedure or nonintervention. In this respect, the humanities in general have provided a broader basis than medicine alone in handling fragile and potentially disastrous confrontations between physicians and patients. The implementation of these ideas over the past twenty years might not have averted conflicts that end up in the courts, but they have allowed a broader public participation in the workings of medical professionals.

In addition, students at the undergraduate level should be taking courses in the sciences, so that the comparison between the "sciences" and the "humanities" will be part of their intellectual background and orientation. When a balanced undergraduate education is fulfilled, there will be a difference in medical training between those devoted exclusively to research and those involved in caring for patients. One may argue that the two are intimately connected so that any separation in the training of physicians will undermine the strength of both sorts of physicians. However, I think that this issue ought to be brought to light and discussed openly during medical school training only and not before that time, so that no preconceived ideas will dominate possible changes in individual attitudes.

In light of such broad undergraduate training, medical school students should be separated into two groups— those focusing on research and those focusing on patient care. The measurement of communication skills and personality traits found to be helpful in the interaction between patients and physicians (cf., Napodano 1986, 96–107) could be used to help separate qualified students into the two different categories. Those focused on research should continue their scientific training, but now with increased doses of philosophy, sociology, and politics of science. They should be introduced to the scientific community in terms of the communal characteristics it displays—notions of group cooperation, rivalry, competition, publication chances, grants awards, and other such issues should be discussed and studied at length. Such education could reduce the number of cases where fraud is detected and could ensure a more fulfilling atmosphere of lifelong commitment than is currently enjoyed by most researchers.

As for those choosing to focus on provision of health care, it seems that the first two years of "scientific" training currently provided in most medical schools is unnecessary because it is deceptive. Claiming to train and prepare students for the use of medical jargon in the future, these science courses are primarily used to "weed out" the "weak" minds—those minds not capable of mastering "scientific data" and scientific "methods"—those privileged portions of the general intellectual reservoir. These science courses are also deceptive when they present a consensus view of science and the scientific world, rather than explore competing models, frameworks, and methods of inquiry. For example, does a physician use the inductive or deductive model? (The question may be improperly phrased altogether, for in most cases they use both simultaneously.)

If the intent is to imbue students with analytical skills, this can be accomplished by teaching either logic or literary criticism; if the intent is to teach the appropriate function of pharmaceutical drugs, many biochemical courses are quite useless, since they are either too elementary or too in-depth for practical use. This becomes most obvious when we realize that current research in biomedicine is developing so rapidly that medical students cannot be expected to keep up with all the latest developments. On the other hand, if medical school is supposed to prepare students to become physicians, then so-called peripheral courses, commonly known as electives (Jones 1985), should become part of the basic curriculum. In addition, physicians are properly taught to be clinicians through the apprenticeship method. This method, as most medical school professors would agree, should not be at the end of training but should be prominent from the very beginning (recalling the Platonic sense of the art of medicine, a technique, a skill one masters while practicing it).

OPENING MEDICAL DISCOURSE TO CRITICISM

Some of these proposals may seem unwarranted and obviously the brainchild of a philosopher, maybe one who never needed any medical attention. Yet it seems that patients would care less about the "correct" use of a Latin term than they would about the interaction that takes place between them and medical institutions. To some extent, the refutation of the hypothesis in question (concerning the link between ethical dilemmas and the education of physicians) might be impossible, since it requires too radical a change in the curriculum of medical schools. In another sense, even if some ethical dilemmas are traceable to overly scientific training or a lack of sensitivity or communication skills, there is no guarantee that all of them would be eliminated were the training of medical professionals to change.

Yet, I have argued that ethical dilemmas in medicine have everything to do with the presumed authority of physicians in light of the presumed authority of scientific knowledge (Ormiston and Sassower 1990). Even when uncertainties are acknowledged, the decision-making process, as Michael Katz reminds us, still revolves around medical scientific questions and not around some technical devices the medical institutions have been able to master over the years.

When one goes to a Chinese doctor, say an acupuncturist, one could care less about the theoretical underpinnings of the practice, about the philosophical principles that guide that specific model. What one cares about are the answers to the simple questions: Does it work? and Will this work for me? Once the theoretical pretense has been avoided, there is no room for medical authority as such and definitely not an authority exerted through institutional channels. Instead, all that is left is technical skill, the ability to make a difference, to change the course of one's ailment or suffering. Whether or not such difference can be accounted for through so-called scientific data is a secondary issue. There will be, it seems, plenty of room and even respect for the technical prowess of this or that medical practitioner. But such respect is no different that the respect one has for the skill with which an electrician performs a task or the skill with which a theatrical play is staged (cf., Schwartz 1981).

Medicine should be considered a technology, a technique, or a set of techniques with a heritage, a tradition, or even an inductive justification (methodologically speaking). As such, the languages of medicine are conventions that turn out to "work well" for a particular purpose under certain conditions. That is, no matter how relativistic they may turn out to be on epistemological or metaphysical grounds, their pragmatic strength or efficacy can account for their public acceptance. Conversely, deficiencies, failures, and repeated mistakes, unless revised and modified, account for public suspicion or outright rejection (including lawsuits). Medical academics could spearhead the effort to translate the professional language to a language everyone can understand and ensure professional modesty and accessibility.

In this sense, then, the medical discourse, understood here to include not only the language of medicine as it appears in professional journals and health care institutions but also its educational practices, would benefit from relinquishing its claims to authority. Remaining open to critical evaluation and to different modes of interpretation, it would increase its popularity with an eager public that needs to rely on medicine as it gradually ages. As life expectancy has increased from forty-seven years at the beginning of the twentieth century to seventy-six by its end, health care has become more, rather than less, important in all of our daily lives. Our reliance, then, on medicine has increased; our expectations that it will deliver cures to all our ailments have increased; our funding of medical research has increased. Can we expect in return an increased sensitivity and openness?

5

+

Academics as Visionaries and Prophets

A VISION OF THEIR OWN

My plea throughout this book, regardless of the few digressions I have taken the liberty to offer, is the promotion of the life of the mind. The life of the mind is a label we have given to any and all intellectual activity whose fruits are not immediately evident. This is a life that can be as active as the life of commerce, as challenging as the life of the body or as athletic life, and as demanding as any practical ordeal in which we are involved. What distinguishes the life of the mind from the rest of life is not its difficulty or intrigue but rather the elusiveness of its rewards. The rewards of intellectual activity are not necessarily tangible goods. You cannot always immediately assess the results of the life of the mind because the results may not be realized for generations. And finally, the internal reward of living a fulfilling intellectual life comes to some in the form of peace of mind, a tranquil state of being that is hard to detect and even harder to define.

My plea, then, is first and foremost to intellectuals themselves or those who are training to be intellectuals—students. In a climate where the life of the mind is paramount and where internal curiosity drives people to lose sleep because a new idea just popped into their heads or because an old problem cannot be resolved, in this climate the quest for tenure, for example, becomes inconsequential. The worry over tenure and salary raises, about job security and the life of luxury, should be worries reserved for those outside the academy, for those who are supposed to fund the academy. If you accept my initial plea for legislators and the public (chapter 1) to view the academy as one of our welfare systems, then my plea would seem quite reasonable.

I know well the debates over tenure and freedom of speech, the protection of long-term research projects, and the ability to be critical in face of fascist regimes. But if my model were to be properly understood by responsible academics and a generous culture that needs its future shielded from poor choices by greedy capitalists, it would take care of all these issues. My welfare model of the sanctuary of higher learning would ensure a protection wider than tenure and an open-mindedness the Bill of Rights and the U.S. Constitution could not spell out in enough detail. Finally, my view of the sanctuary as a response to the emerging model would also provide a vision for what the academy should be about.

The notion of a vision statement has become banal and vague in the hands of academic administrators who want to streamline intellectual life to the limits of public expectations. But visions do make a difference, and prophetic ideas can transform a society. I would venture to say that the public knows that this is the case! But will the public pay to hear criticism? Does the public tolerate, let alone revere those who dare speak out against their own conduct and set of beliefs? It seems that while expecting intellectuals to warn us against future catastrophes and provide the tools with which to overcome them, we may not want to waste precious funds on idle thinking and "pure" science (as opposed to "applied" science).

The emerging model of the academy, where a few research centers do the thinking for society as a whole while the rest of the thousands of institutions of higher education provide minimal skill training, responds to one pressure: let's not waste time and money on the life of the mind. The other pressure that explains the extent to which the life of the mind is necessary for the survival of the entire (political) body is not always heard as loudly as we would hope it would be. If the emerging model of the academy seems to fall short of providing us with survival tools for the future, then perhaps it would urge us all to accept the essential role academics and intellectuals (who overlap only some of the time) play in furthering the well-being of humanity. Intellectuals could thrive in their newly found cultural role, in my view, only if we implemented the third welfare system and established my sanctuary model.

PUBLIC VERSUS PRIVATE KNOWLEDGE

The deconstruction and reconstruction of epistemologies or theories of knowledge (what we know and how we know what we claim to know) over the past few decades indicate a multiplicity of perspectives and methods of inquiry. Whether called Marxists or Popperians, feminists or postmodernists, different academic groups share some theoretical commitments that are overlooked during their epistemological and political squabbles with each other.

I propose to indicate some common themes and concerns not so much in order to obliterate the differences between these perspectives, but rather in order to strengthen their political effectiveness in dealing with the public. This is a public that might figure out, as I am arguing here, that the life of the mind is important and that listening to academics is important. I am concerned here not with "party" lines (in terms of the different academic disciplines) and agendas (in terms of scholarly disputes and institutional power plays) but instead with the provision of intellectual choices to the public at large and to those initiated into the intellectual arena.

Being a philosopher by training, I think it most appropriate to include what sociologists call a reflexive moment, one that puts my own intellectual conduct within the parameters of my critical comments. With this in mind, I offer this closing chapter as a recommendation (rather than an argument) for those of us who consider themselves students of the culture in which we live and think, a culture the distinction of which is associated with the scientific enterprise (from architecture to medicine).

The recommendation is quite simple: incorporate and integrate a variety of critical perspectives to accomplish your specified tasks, instead of quarreling with each other to the extent that you preempt the potential for change. The unifying theme of all critics, if one can find one, is their posture vis-à-vis the scientific establishment, that is, a deep-rooted belief in being antiestablishment. The posture is not always limited to outright antagonism; there are also attempts to contribute a critical perspective that will enhance internal changes of the scientific establishment. As a working definition, one may conceive of the scientific establishment as being located within large-scale research centers within private industry and the academy and extensively sponsored by government agencies, such as the National Science Foundation, the National Institutes of Health, and the Defense Department.

My recommendation for a concerted effort to incorporate a variety of critiques is at once too simple and not simple enough. Too simple in the sense of overlooking histories and differences underlying a certain way of philosophizing; not simple enough in the sense of not specifying in detail what the next move(s) ought to be. In this respect, then, those philosophers, politicians, and prejudiced individuals already committed politically to this or that school might not listen to me, might not even hear the story I tell. But perhaps other people who have not yet made up their minds or who are disillusioned with a particular school, will discover in my stories something they would like to listen to.

THE EMERGING MODEL REVISITED

The emerging model of higher education that has served as the backdrop for this book is a model I would like not to see followed to its completion. Why would we want to have only ten to twenty well-funded research institutions as our brain trust, while the rest of the land is peppered with lower-end teaching schools for remedial training and low-level mastery of basic skills? In the land of opportunity, the land of upward mobility and Yankee ingenuity, we would expect more access to more knowledge for more citizens. If indeed 10 to 20 percent of our population is enrolled in institutions of higher education at any given time, and if these institutions are supposed to inspire and not simply train us to read and write and think critically, then we should fight to revamp the emerging model.

Perhaps I can summarize most simply my deep belief in the contribution of philosophy to the life of the mind (beyond any particular adherence to this or that world-view), and the contribution it can make to revamping the emerging narrow model of higher education. As far as I can tell, in order to plead for the life of the mind, as already indicated at the beginning of this chapter, I must also convince legislators to fund a sanctuary for intellectuals. This sanctuary has to prove useful to legislators in some sense, otherwise they would reject out of hand any proposal to sanction yet another welfare system. I say sanction rather than create, since I believe that the welfare system of the mind is already in place in one form or another but is not fully funded or fully appreciated as such.

Let me suggest three tenets that may form the basis of this sanctuary, the trinity of practices of the mind that would enhance the life of the mind in the sanctuary of the academy. First, we need to question every assumption that is presented to us, no matter how sacred it has become in our culture. Tradition tends to create habits of the mind that obscure problems and gloss over difficulties, and we must combat this human tendency. Second, we need to define as carefully as possible every term, notion, and concept with which we work. Careless use of undefined terms can bring about confusions, misunderstanding, and even war. And third, we must carefully compose our arguments and follow their steps with rigor and attention. Faulty reasoning is harmful not only for the individual who practices logic but for any member of a community who tries to communicate with others.

We must remember that the appeal to uniformity (linguistically speaking) has some great advantages that get lost in the critique of hegemonic dominance. The sanctuary I envision could accommodate as many perspectives as possible and could tolerate as many contradictory views so long as they could be presented cogently and understood cognitively by all participants. These three principles, or tenets, could provide a starting point for the establishment of a model for the life of the mind. It would leave open the possibility for speculation and inspiration, because some level of agreement could already be achieved.

From a different angle, the question of the life of the mind is not limited to linguistic prowess and logical craftiness or to lofty speculations. I am not advocating intellectual laziness (exercises in logic) or feeblemindedness (stream of consciousness) as an escape from worldly activities and the engagement with nature and humanity. I am not advocating the setting of privileged sanctuaries for academics so that they can hide from the challenges of their day. Instead, I plead for academic sanctuaries where individuals could cooperate and help each other to develop new alternatives to age-old problems (rather than compete with each other for financial rewards). I plead for places where the pressures of daily survival give rise to long-term solutions. In short, I plead for places where we can leapfrog present calamities to avert future disasters.

On the question of collaboration, we should pay attention to the kind of collaboration we find on factory floors and in research laboratories in medical schools and corporate centers. Perhaps what is at issue is the notion of division of labor, already advocated more than two hundred years ago by Adam Smith. Perhaps what is at issue is the sheer size of projects so that no individual can do the job alone. In the contemporary age of Big Science, where the assembly of a car, the building of a large skyscraper, or the construction of an atomic bomb are the standard fare, there is no sense in which any individual can master the whole project. The arts and crafts of yesteryear have given way to the industrial revolution and large-scale production. Given the realities of modern-day technoscience, it would seem reasonable, if not imperative, that all of us, academics included, would feel comfortable to collaborate with each other and those around us (see Sassower 1989). As contemporary businesses appreciate, the collaboration among groups of individuals is a more effective way to use the brainpower of every individual. This way of doing business goes beyond the dichotomy between competition and cooperation and sets the stage for making personal contributions for the group as a whole.

Sigmund Freud taught us between the two world wars that there are two major principles that drive humanity to behave the way it does, two principles he borrowed from his psychoanalytical analysis of individual egos and their development: the pleasure principle and the reality principle (see Freud 1961). It is difficult to generalize from the experiences of one individual ego formation to an entire culture, but Freud craftily explains how the drive for happiness, left unchecked, could turn into excesses that would eventually become harmful. What maintains the individual as well as the culture within the boundaries of reason, or within functional boundaries, is the controls put on the drive for happiness (or libidinal economy). In this context, then, societies have developed norms of conduct and codes of behavior (also known as ethics) in order to preserve the well-being of all individuals within a community.

The academics or intellectuals on which I rely here must not only appreciate all of these issues as they have emerged over the past two thousand years of recorded Western history, but must also become role models for the entire population. In this respect, academics, despite their sanctuary, have a leadership role that is exemplified in the positions they hold as much as in whatever specific ideas they lecture about or write down and publish. In order to be intellectual leaders, they must have at least three characteristics. (Incidentally, if they conform to adopting and maintaining these characteristics, they could also more effectively ensure the retention of their sanctuary amidst the demands of commerce and industry.) First, they have to embody an intellectual curiosity and thirst for life's full-ness that would make them active, engaged, and willing participants in the life of the mind. Second, they must have integrity, be honest, and humble. These personal traits or qualities could protect them from being seduced by immediate gratification, fame, and money. And third, they must be willing to belong to a community of scholars and researchers as opposed to maintaining fierce competi-tive independence.

I wish to distinguish here between one's autonomy, the willingness to have courage to say whatever seems to be the truth, and a sense of independence that claims that no other people are needed for the survival of this particular member of the species. This distinction is another way of reiterating my concern for some level of collaboration among the leaders and role models of the culture so that the culture as a whole would be more receptive to collabo-ration. If these three sets of characteristics are found in those seeking the sanctuary of the academy, then we could hope for a better future in the face of our current situation.

PARTING COMMENTS

This book has been about academics, the faculties of insti-tutions of higher education, and not about students. This book has been about the emergence of an academic model that would serve poorly the needs of these faculties. And finally, this book has been about the provision of a sanc-tuary for intellectuals so that in their collaboration they could further the well-being of society as a whole. In short, this book could be read as yet another self-serving treatise on the need to protect academics from the pressures of commercialized technoscience. But this is not exactly what I had in mind when first proposing to write this book. So, let me review what I think is at stake for the next century when it comes to the well-being of our Western culture. In doing so, I will refrain from making lofty claims about the importance of knowledge and the cross-fertilization of future generations. Instead, I will stick to simple and straightforward ideas to which I hope we can all subscribe.

First, in the information age we are concerned with knowledge claims and the criteria by which to distinguish important and relevant knowledge claims from claims that have no informative content at all. In other words, we are worried about the "garbage in" problem, because no matter how ingenious our technological devices, we want to avoid receiving "garbage out." Only with critical training can we ensure that we have enough gatekeepers around our knowledge centers and around the devices with which we collect, process, and analyze data.

Second, we need to train people to be critical, since simply discarding everything is not the same as being critical. Academic institutions could fulfill this task as intellectual sanctuaries where enough databases are stored and processed, where numerous alternatives are always developed, and where there is an ongoing questioning of the criteria by which we judge one set of ideas or principles to be superior to another. This does not mean that either "anything goes" or that only "my way is the right way" (if said by a senior tenured professor). Rather, this means that we find ourselves struggling along a continuum of ideas and principles, a continuum of criteria, and the ever-changing cultural environment within which the whole process takes place.

Third, now that we have suggested why critical analysis is important and where this skill can be best studied, we should focus on those who can provide this valuable service as well as be role models of how this critical process unfolds. You see, by now I have come around to what I call intellectual refugees who find sanctuary in the academy. They avoid the temptations of commerce and industry, even though their skills could be useful there; they avoid the quick fixes and short-terms gains that are readily available. And they find solace in knowing that even their most fruitful ideas and inventions may sometime find an application that would improve the living conditions of society and perhaps enhance their own reputation.

Understood in these terms, then, I can move to the fourth point, namely, the twofold pressure put on intellectuals in their sanctuary. On the one hand, they have to accept the fact that society will wish to be compensated for the financial support given to the academic sanctuary. On the other hand, they have their own internal pressure to eschew the pressure of the world external to their sanctuary. The predicament is obvious: how to concede enough to the public without being enslaved to its whims. I'm not sure there is an easy way out of this predicament, for the engagement with the public is essential if academics are going to have anything useful to say to or do for the public. On the other hand, the whole idea of having a sanctuary is so that academics will not be influenced by the political waves that wash on the shores of culture, may they be fascist or others. So, which side should we prefer?

In order to retain the promise of a long-term vision to solve short-term problems and in order to be able to recall and recycle ancient ideas and practices because of their potential effectiveness, I would suggest that we shield academics from unnecessary pressures. How do we define unnecessary compared to necessary pressures? Unnecessary are those quick-fix ones that may satisfy a customer today but that will not get deep enough to recognize an underlying problem. Necessary pressures are those pressures that remind academics that someone is willing to subsidize them and that therefore they have an added responsibility to do more with their time and intelligence, with their skills and knowledge. This would not mean that waste would be eliminated, since some sort of academic waste is essential for creative production (corporate America agrees with this, incidentally, and provides panoramic vistas to engineers and outdoor activities for management teams). But we can be responsible with the funds allocated to us, be mindful that there are great expectations concerning our alleged brilliance and superior intelligence.

So, as we recognize that we know less, as we are humbled by the life of the mind, we should continue to explain to ourselves and others that the small steps we take on the journey to wisdom are important and limited but hold an incredible promise for the future. In some ways, we are casino proprietors and managers asking the patrons to gamble their hard-earned money on the promise of great riches. The difference, of course, is that the house fixes the odds against all patrons, while we, as academics, have no control over fixing any odds or over the outcome of any research project. Our inherent innocence should not be lost on us or on the public; our curiosity and integrity should be the seductive elements in the flirtation between the life of the mind and the life of the body. While Freud offered the reality principle as a moderating tool for the unbridled conquests of the pleasure principle, I offer the life of the mind as a necessary (if not sufficient) condition with which to enhance the life of the body.

One could say that my offer runs contrary to Freud's, since I wish to excite the body through the mind rather than limit its appetite. But perhaps my plea is more ancient than Freud's. I believe that the life of the mind has the power to transform, redirect, and even excite a body that has been left to wander in the forest of teasing entities, none of which is accompanied by explanatory models that would be useful in choosing between alternatives. To believe that there are no alternatives is silly, and to believe that the choices are simple and clear is also silly; so what is needed is the intellectual intervention to explain critical analyses and even justify the choices we make within an ever-increasing set of alternatives. Only then can we make ourselves useful as intellectuals and avoid prejudices (pre-judgements) of all sorts. The seduction of the life of the mind will result in an improved body and eventually in a sophisticated, tolerant, and interesting culture.

References

Agassi, Joseph. 1963. *Towards an Historiography of Science. Beiheft 2, History and Theory*. Middletown, Conn.: Wesleyan University Press.

————. 1975. *Science in Flux*. Dordrecht: D. Reidel.

————. 1981. *Science and Society: Studies in the Sociology of Science*. Dordrecht: D. Reidel.

————. 1985. *Technology: Philosophical and Social Aspects*. Dordrecht: D. Reidel.

Agassi, Joseph, and I. C. Jarvie, eds. 1987. *Rationality: The Critical View*. Dordrecht: Martinus Nijhoff Publishers.

Amrine, Frederick, Francis J. Zucker, and Harvey Wheeler, eds. 1987. *Goethe and the Sciences: A Reappraisal*. Dordrecht: D. Reidel.

Aronowitz, Stanley, and William DiFaizo. 1995. *The Jobless Future*. Minneapolis: University of Minnesota Press.

Aronowitz, Stanley, and Henry A. Giroux. 1991. *Postmodern Education: Politics, Culture, and Social Criticism*. Minneapolis: University of Minnesota Press.

Atwood, Margaret. 1985. *Handmaid's Tale*. New York: Doubleday.

Barbour, Ian G. 1966. *Issues in Science and Religion*. Englewood Cliffs, N.J.: Prentice-Hall.

Berkson, William, and John Wettersten. 1984. *Learning from Error: Karl Popper's Psychology of Learning*. La Salle, Ill.: Open Court.

Bledstein, Burton J. 1976. *The Culture of Professionalism: The Middle Class and the Development of Higher Education in America*. New York: W.W. Norton.

Bloom, Allan. 1987. *The Closing of the American Mind: How Higher Education has Failed Democracy and Impoverished the Souls of Today's Students*. New York: Simon and Schuster.

Boggs, Carl. 1993. *Intellectuals and the Crisis of Modernity*. Albany: State University of New York Press.

Bok, Derek. 1982. *Beyond the Ivory Tower: Social Responsibilities of the Modern University*. Cambridge, Mass.: Harvard University Press.

Bourdieu, Pierre. 1988. *Homo Academicus* [1984], trans. Peter Collier. Stanford, Calif.: Stanford University Press.

Boyer, Ernest L. 1987. *College: The Undergraduate Experience in America*. New York: Harper and Row.

Bynum, J., and G. Sheets. 1985. "Medical School Socialization and the New Physician: Role, Status, Adjustments, Personal Problems, and Social Identity," *Psychological Reports* 57, 182.

Castells, Manuel, Ramon Flecha, Paulo Freire, Henry A. Giroux, Donaldo Macedo, and Paul Willis. 1999. *Critical Education in the New Information Age*. Lanham, Md.: Rowman & Littlefield Publishers.

Clark, Evert. "Where Have All the High-Tech Teachers Gone? As Science and Engineering Professors Retire in Droves, A Crisis Brews," *Business Week* (1/27/86), Science & Technology, 103.

Cohen, Robert S., and Marx Wartofsky, eds. 1984. *Hegel and the Sciences*. Dordrecht: D. Reidel.

Cohen, Sande. 1993. *Academia and the Luster of Capital*. Minneapolis: University of Minnesota Press.

Condorcet, Antoine Nicolas de. 1955. *Sketch for a Historical Picture of the Progress of the Human Mind* [1795], trans. June Brarraclough. Westport, Conn: Greenwood Press.

Dewey, John. 1960. *The Quest for Certainty: A Study of the Relation of Knowledge and Action* [1929]. New York: G. P. Putnam.

Duhem, Pierre. 1990. *German Science*. La Salle,Ill.: Open Court.

Engelhardt, H. T. Jr. 1986. *The Foundations of Bioethics*. New York: Oxford University Press.

Feyerabend, Paul. 1978. *Science in a Free Society*. London: NLB.

Fleck, Ludwig. 1979. *Genesis and Development of a Scientific Fact* [1935]. Chicago: University of Chicago Press.

Foucault, Michel. 1971. *Madness and Civilization* [1961], trans. Richard Howard. New York: Vintage.

———. 1979. *Discipline and Punish: The Birth of the Prison* [1975], trans. Alan Sheridan. New York: Vintage.

Freire, Paulo. 1972. *Pedagogy of the Oppressed* [1968], trans. Myra Bergman Ramos. New York: Herder & Herder.

———. 1985. *The Politics of Education: Culture, Power, and Liberation*, trans. Donaldo Macedo. South Hadley, Mass.: Bergin & Garvey.

———. 1998. *Pedagogy of Freedom: Ethics, Democracy, and Civic Courage*, trans. Patrick Clarke. Lanham, Md.: Rowman & Littlefield.

Freud, Sigmund. 1961. *Civilization and Its Discontent* [1929], trans. and ed. James Strachey. New York: W.W. Norton.

Galton, Francis. 1869. *Hereditary Genius*. Magnolia, Mass.: Peter Smith Publisher (1990).

Gellner, Ernest. 1992. *Reason and Culture: The Historic Role of Rationality and Rationalism*. Oxford: Blackwell.

Giroux, Henry A. 1983. *Theory and Resistance in Education: A Pedagogy for the Opposition*. South Hadley, Mass.: Bergin & Garvey.

———. 1988. *Schooling and the Struggle for Public Life: Critical Pedagogy in the Modern Age*. Minneapolis: University of Minnesota Press.

Gouldner, Alvin W. 1982. *The Future of Intellectuals and the Rise of the New Class: A Frame of Reference, Theses, Conjectures, Arguments, and an Historical Perspective on the Role of Intellectuals and Intelligentsia in the International Class Contest of the Modern Era* [1979]. New York: Oxford University Press.

Graber, Robert Bates. 1995. *Valuing Useless Knowledge: An Anthropological Inquiry into the Meaning of Liberal Education*. Kirksville, Mo.: Thomas Jefferson University Press.

Gross, Paul R., and Norman Levitt. 1994. *Higher Superstition: The Academic Left and Its Quarrels with Science*. Baltimore: Johns Hopkins University Press.

Hall, Stuart. 1992. "Cultural Studies and Its Theoretical Legacies." In *Cultural Studies*, edited by Lawrence Grossberg, Cary Nelson, and Paula Treichler, pp. 277–94. New York: Routledge.

Hirsch, E. D. Jr. 1987. *Cultural Literacy: What Every American Needs to Know*. Boston: Houghton Mifflin.

Hoekema, David A. 1994. *Campus Rules and Moral Community: In Place of Loco Parentis*. Lanham, Md.: Rowman & Littlefield Publishers.

Hoesterey, Ingeborg, ed. 1991. *Zeitgeist in Babel: The Postmodernist Controversy*. Bloomington: Indiana University Press.

Hofstadter, Richard. 1962. *Anti-Intellectualism in American Life*. New York: Knopf.

Honan, William H. 1996. "Minnesota's Proposed Tenure Changes Lead to Union Drive," *New York Times* (9/22/96), C17.

Ibsen, Henrik. 1882. *An Enemy of the People*. New York: New American Library.

Illich, Ivan. 1970. *Deschooling Society.* New York: Harper & Row.

Jones, K. V. 1985. "Type A and Academic Performance: A Negative Relationship," *Psychological Reports* 56, 260.

Karabell, Zachary. 1998. *What's College For? The Struggle to Define American Higher Education.* New York: Basic Books.

Katz, Jay. 1984. *The Silent World of Doctors and Patients.* New York: The Free Press.

Katz, Michael B. 1987. *Reconstructing American Education.* Cambridge, Mass.: Harvard University Press.

Kerr, Clark. 1963. *The Uses of the University.* Cambridge, Mass.: Harvard University Press.

Knight, J. A. 1973. *Medical Student: Doctor in the Making.* New York: Appleton-Century-Crofts.

Koeppel, David. 1999. "Education Life," *New York Times* (4/4/99), 29.

Konrad, George, and Ivan Szelenyi. 1979. *The Intellectuals on the Road to Class Power,* trans. Andrew Arato and Richard E. Allen. New York: Harcourt Brace Jovanovich.

Kuhn, Thomas S. 1970. *The Structure of Scientific Revolutions* [1962]. Chicago: University of Chicago Press.

Lang, Fritz. 1924. *Metropolis.*

Laor, Nathaniel, and Joseph Agassi. 1990. *Diagnosis: Philosophical and Medical Perspectives.* Dordrecht: Kluwer Academic Publishers.

Latour, Bruno. 1987. *Science in Action.* Cambridge: Cambridge University Press.

Leatherman, Courtney. 1999. "Growth in Positions off the Tenure Track Is a Trend That's Here to Stay, Study Finds," *The Chronicle of Higher Education* (4/9/99), A16.

Lyotard, Jean-Francoise. 1984. *The Postmodern Condition: A Report on Knowledge* [1979], trans. Geoff Bennington and Brian Massumi. Minneapolis: University of Minnesota Press.

Lyotard, Jean-Francoise, and Jean-Loup Thebaud. 1985. *Just Gaming* [1979], trans. Wlad Godzich. Minneapolis: University of Minnesota Press.

Machell, D. F. 1988. "A Discourse on Professional Melancholia," *Community Review* Vol. 9, 1–2: 41–50.

Machlup, Fritz. 1962. *The Production and Distribution of Knowledge in the United States.* Princeton, N.J.: Princeton University Press.

Maeroff, Gene I. 1993. "College Teachers, the New Leisure Class," *Wall Street Journal* (9/13/93), A12.

Maheux, B., and F. Beland. 1987. "Changes in Students' Sociopolitical Attitudes during Medical School: Socialization or Maturation Effect?" *Social Science and Medicine* 24, 619–24.

Malinowski, Bronislaw. 1948. *Magic, Science and Religion and Other Essays.* New York: Doubleday Anchor Books.

Malthus, Thomas. 1970. *An Essay on the Principles of Population* [1798]. Harmondsworth, Engl.: Penguin Books.

Markie, Peter J. 1994. *Professor's Duties: Ethical Issues in College Teaching.* Lanham, Md.: Rowman & Littlefield Publishers.

McFall, S. L. 1986. "Stress and Social Support in Medical School," Ph.D. Dissertation, University of North Carolina at Chapel Hill.

Menand, Louis. 1996. "How to Make a Ph.D. Matter," *New York Times Magazine* (9/22/1996), 78–81.

Merod, Jim. 1987. *The Political Responsibility of the Critic.* Ithaca, N. Y.: Cornell University Press.

Miller, Matthew. 1999. "$140,000—And a Bargain: College Tuition Has Increased Significantly Faster than Inflation. But There Actually Are Reasons," *The New York Times Magazine* (6/13/99), 48–9.

Mooney, C. J. 1989. "Feeling Disillusioned? Unappreciated? You May Be a Victim of What a Psychologist Describes as 'Professional Melancholia,'" *Chronicle of Higher Education* Vol. 36, 9: 13–14.

Napodano, R. J. 1986. *Values in Medical Practice: A Statement of Philosophy for Physicians and a Model for Teaching a Healing Science.* New York: Human Sciences Press.

Nelson, Cary and Stephen Watt. 1999. *Academic Keywords: A Devil's Dictionary for Higher Education.* New York: Routledge.

Ormiston, Gayle, and Raphael Sassower. 1989. *Narrative Experiments: The Discursive Authority of Science and Technology.* Minneapolis: University of Minnesota Press.

Ormiston, Gayle, and Raphael Sassower, eds. 1990. *Prescriptions: The Dissemination of Medical Authority.* Westport, Conn.: Greenwood Press.

Pascarella, E. T., E. M. Brier, J. C. Smart, and L. Herzog. 1987. "Becoming a Physician: The Influence of the Undergraduate Experience," *Research in Higher Education* 26, 180–201.

Poirier, S., and D. J. Brauner. 1988. "Ethics and the Daily Language of Medical Discourse," *Hastings Center Report* (August/September), 5–9.

Polanyi, Michael. 1969. *Knowing and Being,* edited by Marjorie Grene. Chicago: University of Chicago Press.

Popper, Karl R. 1959. *The Logic of Scientific Discovery* [1935]. New York: Harper & Row.

———. 1972. *Objective Knowledge.* Oxford: Clarendon Press.

Price, Kingsley. 1962. *Education and Philosophical Thought.* Boston: Allyn and Bacon.

Probyn, Elspeth. 1992. "Technologizing the Self: A Future Anterior for Cultural Studies." In *Cultural Studies,* edited by Lawrence Grossberg, Cary Nelson, and Paula Treichler, pp. 501–11.

Reznek, L. 1987. *The Nature of Disease.* London: Routledge and Kegan Paul.

Robins, L. S., and F. M. Wolf. 1988. "Confrontation and Politeness Strategies in Physician-Patient Interaction," *Social Science and Medicine* 27, 217–21.

Ross, Andrew. 1989. *No Respect: Intellectuals and Popular Culture.* New York: Routledge.

Russell, Bertrand. 1935. *Religion and Science.* New York: Henry Holt.

———. 1950. *Unpopular Essays.* New York: Simon and Schuster.

Sassower, Raphael. 1989. "Collaboration as a Pedagogical Device." In *The History and Philosophy of Science in Science Teaching,* edited by Don Emil Herget, pp. 313–21. Tallahassee: Florida State University Press.

———.1990. "Medical Education: The Training of Ethical Physicians," *Studies in Philosophy and Education* 10, 251–61.

———. 1993. *Knowledge without Expertise: On the Status of Scientists.* Albany: Sate University of New York Press.

———. 1994. "On Madness in the Academy," *Journal of Higher Education,* Vol. 65, 4: 473–85.

———. 1995. *Cultural Collisions: Postmodern Technoscience.* New York: Routledge.

———. 1997. "Misplaced Pressure: Between Bondage and Rage at the University," *Science Studies.*

———. 1998. *Technocsientific Angst: Ethics and Responsibility.* Minneapolis: University of Minnesota Press.

Sassower, Raphael, and Michael Grodin. 1987. "Scientific Uncertainty and Medical Responsibility," *Theoretical Medicine* 8, 221–34.

Schachner, Nathan. 1962. *The Mediaeval Universities* [1938]. New York: A. S. Barnes.

Scheffler, Israel. 1973. *Reason and Teaching.* New York: Routledge and Kegan Paul.

Schrecker, Ellen. 1986. *No Ivory Tower: McCarthyism and the Universities.* New York: Oxford University Press.

Schwartz, R. 1981. "Acupuncture and Expertise: A Challenge to Physician Control," *The Hastings Center Report,* (April), 5–7.

Searle, John. 1990. "The Storm over the University," *The New York Review of Books* (10/6/96), 34–42.

Shaw, Bernard. 1906. Preface to *The Doctor's Dilemma* in *The Complete Prefaces of Bernard Shaw* [1965]. London: Paul Hamlyn.

Skoie, Hans. 1996. "Basic Research—A New Funding Climate?" *Science and Public Policy*, Vol. 23, 2:66–75.

Snow, C. P. 1964. *The Two Cultures and a Second Look*. Cambridge: Cambridge University Press.

Sontag, Susan. 1977. *Illness as Metaphor*. New York: Farrar, Straus and Giroux.

———. 1988. *AIDS and Its Metaphors*. New York: Farrar, Straus and Giroux.

Stigler, George J. 1984. *The Intellectual and the Marketplace*. Cambridge: Harvard University Press.

Toulmin, Stephen. 1981. "The Emergence of Post-Modern Science," *The Great Ideas Today*. Chicago: Encyclopedia Britannica.

Uchitelle, Louis. 1996. "Basic Research Is Losing out as Companies Stress Results," *New York Times* (9/8/96), A1, C8.

"U. of California Graduate Students Strike," *New York Times* (11/24/96) B18.

Veblen, Thorstein. 1957. *The Higher Learning in America* [1918]. New York: Wang & Hill.

Virshup, B. 1985. *Coping in Medical Schools*. New York: Norton.

Weber, Samuel. 1987. *Institution and Interpretation*. Minneapolis: University of Minnesota Press.

Weingartner, Rudolph H. 1999. *The Moral Dimensions of Academic Administration*. Lanham, Md.: Rowman & Littlefield Publishers.

Wolff, Robert Paul. 1969. *The Ideal of the University*. Boston: Beacon Press

Index

About the Author

Raphael Sassower is professor of philosophy at the University of Colorado, Colorado Springs. His most recent books include *Cultural Collisions: Postmodern Technoscience* (1995) and *Technoscientific Angst: Ethics and Responsibility* (1998).